D1083453

*Narrative Means to
Therapeutic Ends*

David Epston is a Co-director of The Family Therapy Centre in Auckland, New Zealand. Michael White is a Co-director of the Dulwich Centre, Adelaide, Australia. The authors made different, but equal, contributions to this book.

A NORTON PROFESSIONAL BOOK

Narrative Means to Therapeutic Ends

Michael White   *David Epston*

W.W. NORTON & COMPANY
NEW YORK · LONDON

Printed in the United States of America.

Available in Australia and New Zealand from Dulwich Centre,
345 Carrington Street, Adelaide, Sth Australia 5000, Australia

Library of Congress Cataloging-in-Publication Data

White, Michael.
    Narrative means to therapeutic ends / Michael White, David Epston.
        p.   cm.
    "A Norton professional book."
    Includes bibliographical references.
    1. Letter-writing — Therapeutic use.   2. Psychotherapy.
I. Epston, David.   II. Title.
RC489.W75W47   1990   616.89′166 — dc20   89-48776

    ISBN: 0-393-70098-4

W. W. Norton & Company, Inc., 500 Fifth Avenue, New York, N.Y. 10110
W. W. Norton & Company Ltd., 37 Great Russell Street, London WC1B 3NU

1 2 3 4 5 6 7 8 9 0

Contents

Foreword

Breaking new ground in any field is a major accomplishment. To do so in different directions at the same time and, in so doing, to open up whole new territories reflect a *tour de force*. In my opinion, Michael White and David Epston are engaged in just this kind of trailblazing for the field of family therapy. This compact book represents a distillate of some of their major achievements. It charts a series of bold strides in their reconnaissance into the domain of human problems and stakes out some original therapeutic contributions.

White and Epston are both extremely gifted clinicians, each with his own unique style, but with much in common. Their synergistic collaboration over the last few years has been unusually productive in generating a wide range of new ideas and methods. They have already had a major impact on the clinical practice of many professionals in their home countries of Australia and New Zealand, and now their influence is being felt in the international family therapy scene as well. Since encountering their work three years ago, my own therapeutic methods have changed enormously. Because of the "new trail" they have broken, I have been able to enter into some entirely new domains of practice. Needless to say, this has been extremely gratifying both professionally and personally. Many of my friends and colleagues are having similar experiences. In other words, Epston and White are not only extending their own clinical understanding and skill into new areas but enabling other therapists to do so as well.

But just what are these new territories that Epston and White have been exploring and are inviting us into? In my opinion, the single most important domain that White has opened is that of "externalizing the problem." When the distinction of the problem can be clearly separated from the distinction of the person, it becomes possible to carefully examine the dynamics and direction of the interaction between persons and problems. One can then address a crucial question: Is the problem gaining more influence over the person or is the person gaining more influence over the problem? An in-depth theoretical exploration of this question has led White to reveal not only the oppressive effects of the manner in which problems are typically described, but also the constitutive and subjugating effects of descriptive knowledge itself. In so doing, he has entered the awesome territory of ontology and epistemology. While this aspect of our lives may seem extremely remote and perhaps a bit intimidating to some of us, we are implicitly grounded in it at all times. For instance, our personal identities are constituted by what we "know" about ourselves and how we describe ourselves as persons. But what we know about ourselves is defined, for the most part, by the cultural practices (of describing, labeling, classifying, evaluating, segregating, excluding, etc.) in which we are embedded. As human beings in language, we are, in fact, all subjugated by invisible social "controls" of presuppositional linguistic practices and implicit sociocultural patterns of coordination. In other words, if family members, friends, neighbors, coworkers, and professionals think of a person as "having" a certain characteristic or problem, they exercise "power" over him or her by "performing" this knowledge with respect to that person. Thus, in the social domain, knowledge and power are inextricably interrelated.

In exploring and explicating these complex issues, White draws heavily from the philosophical analysis of modern history by Foucault. Indeed, one of the most important original contributions of this book is White's analysis of Foucault's perspective and its relevance to therapy. This is offered in the first chapter which is, in fact, a major theoretical statement covering a number of important areas. The most significant of these, however, is the discussion of "knowledge as power"—a vast territory that is only beginning to be explored by family therapists. In this statement White is essentially extending his pioneering work on externalizing problems. He does this by disclosing how "knowledge techniques" inadvertently disempower persons and may empower problems in the process. When these covert techniques (such as collapsing problematic descriptions onto persons) can be identified, it becomes much easier to externalize problems and to coordinate a person's escape from them.

The second major territory that Epston and White open for us in this book is the multiplicity of ways in which the written word may be employed therapeutically. This is the land of *Narrative Means to Therapeutic Ends*, and comprises the remaining content of the book. White and Epston offer an incredibly diverse and rich sampling of therapeutic initiatives "in black and white." Using brief case vignettes, they provide numerous inspiring examples of therapeutic letters, invitations, references, certificates, predictions, declarations, etc. As readers, we are free to pick and choose among a variety of new interventions (as we reap the fruits of a new area that has already been carefully ploughed, watered, and weeded for us). The manifold examples bear rereading and careful study to glean the full harvest. Indeed, I suspect that many readers will find themselves drawn back into this territory again and again as they begin to discover how fertile it can be for their own clinical work.

David Epston, in particular, places a great deal of emphasis on the therapeutic potential of routine letters that summarize each session. He has disciplined himself to write a letter to the client or family after almost every interview. The carbon copy of the letter usually constitutes his only written record of the session. In this way the clinical "file" is virtually shared by both the family and the therapist. This pattern of practice constitutes a significant foray into a more egalitarian relationship between professional and client.

What is most intriguing about the Epston and White letters is their fascinating content and style. They are far from being simple "objective" descriptions. The content is carefully selected to bring forth distinctions that are liable to be heuristic, to link specific experiences and events that promise to be resourceful, and to promote those kinds of "stories" that have healing potential. The style tends to employ the subjunctive mood and to rely heavily on the use of vernacular language. Common words and phrases are used in uncommon ways. This generates an enticing novelty that stimulates the reader's imagination and participation in the text.

For instance, a sentence like "A guilt-driven life is a life sentence" can be arresting, while the juxtaposition of contrasting statements like "getting into trouble and become more troubled . . . or . . . getting out of trouble and becoming untroubled" can tantalize the experience of choice. This style of writing is unusually gripping, even for an "outside" reader whose life is not directly involved.

In an attempt to provide a conceptual framework for their exploration of narrative means, Epston and White have drawn on the notion of "narrative texts." They propose the analogy of therapy as a process of "storying" and/or "re-storying" the lives and experiences of persons who present with problems. In other words, by documenting selective events and meanings "in black and white," therapeutic letters and certificates contribute in a very concrete manner to the co-creation of new, liberating narratives. The analogy has a great deal of intuitive appeal and serves to add a great deal of liveliness and drama to the lives of persons included in the narrative.

The analogy of narrative text also serves as a readily traversable bridge between the territory of narrative means and the territory of knowledge as power. Not only do we, as humans, give meaning to our experience by "storying" our lives, but we are also empowered to "perform" our stories through our knowledge of them. Stories can, of course, be liabilities as well as assets. For instance, most of us have a multiplicity of stories available to us about ourselves, about others, and about our relationships. Some of these stories promote competence and wellness. Others serve to constrain, trivialize, disqualify, or otherwise pathologize ourselves, others, and our relationships. Still other stories can be reassuring, uplifting, liberating, revitalizing, or healing. The particular story that prevails or dominates in giving meaning to the events of our lives determines, to a large extent, the nature of our lived experience and our patterns of action. When a problem-saturated story predominates, we are repeatedly invited into disappointment and misery. Given the natural conservative drifting that we are all subject to, it becomes increasingly difficult to liberate ourselves from habitually re-performing the same old problematic story. It is this domination of problematic knowledge and the tenacious prevalence of pathologizing stories that make the exploration of "knowledge as power" so relevant.

Epston and White are inviting us to ask ourselves: How can we enable the writing of personal and collective stories that liberate and heal when the dominant stories are so problem-saturated? In publishing this book, they are sharing some of their discoveries in relation to this question. How ready are we to join them in these explorations and to empower ourselves with some skill in narrative means that might help enliven the lives of our clients and their families?

Karl Tomm, M.D.
The University of Calgary,
Faculty of Medicine

Acknowledgments

We would like to thank the following persons for their helpful comments on an earlier draft of this book, and for their encouragement and support: Ann Epston, Susi Chamberlain, Michael Durrant, Greg Smith, Karl Tomm, and Cheryl White.

Special thanks is due to Jane Hales of Dulwich Centre for typesetting this material and for her tireless and patient response to the many alterations that have been made in the process of writing this book.

Introduction

The inspiration for putting this book together originally came from David Epston. He initially suggested that Dulwich Centre Publications produce an edition of the Dulwich Centre Review devoted to the use of letters in therapy. Cheryl White's enthusiasm for the idea encouraged us to consider the project and to put the time aside to provide a frame for the material. The outcome is this book.

Although David and I had already exchanged some correspondence, I didn't really encounter his work until 1981. This occurred at the Second Australian Family Therapy Conference in Adelaide. I wasn't booked into his workshop and arrived about half an hour after it had started, drawn by the enthusiastic comments of some of the members of the program committee. I was immediately intrigued by what I heard and by the manner in which the material was being presented. I also thought that I recognized certain correspondences in our respective ideas and practices. We talked afterwards, and this marked the beginning of our friendship and professional association.

Since that time, David has continued to enchant workshop audiences in Australia and New Zealand with his stories, and he has successfully encouraged a generation of therapists to extend the storytelling tradition. In so doing, I believe that he has made a central contribution to what can be discerned as a unique "Down Under" therapy style. Many have been introduced to this tradition and style through the "Story Corner" section of the *Australian and New Zealand Journal of Family Therapy*. David has coordinated this section since its inception, and it has continued to be the most popular regular feature of this journal.

David has consistently applied the story of analogy in novel ways to a wide range of presenting problems. Details of this are available in a number of his published works (e.g. Epston, 1983, 1984a, 1985a, 1985b, 1986a, 1986b, 1986c; Epston & Whitney, 1988; Barlow et al., 1987).

Without doubt, David's fascinating childhood experiences (Epston, 1984b) and his former career as an anthropologist ideally equip him to traffic in storytelling. In fact, upon reflecting on his unique location in the therapy world, I see that he hasn't departed from anthropology at all. An anthropological degree has been defined as an "intellectual poaching licence" – an apt description of the sort of credential that David would take most seriously. He collects ideas for stories from all over and displays a profound disrespect for "disciplinary" boundaries in his search for helpful metaphors to interpret events in social systems.

I had been greatly encouraged to consider the story analogy by David, as well as Cheryl White, whose enthusiasm for this analogy came from her readings in feminism. In response to this, I found that the notions derived from the story analogy or, more broadly speaking, the text analogy fit with notions I had derived from the epistemology of anthropologist Gregory Bateson, whose work has interested me for some considerable time.

In our therapeutic endeavors, David and I have been experimenting with written practices for some considerable time. We have accepted the proposition that spoken and written languages have different domains of existence, although we do acknowledge that there is considerable overlap. We believe that the written tradition contributes an extra dimension to our work with persons who experience troublesome problems. The feedback we have received about these practices from those who have sought therapy has reinforced our efforts. We will continue to review and explore ways of extending our use of narrative and written means.

As David and I are geographically separated by several thousand kilometers (David lives in Auckland, New Zealand and I live in Adelaide, South Australia), most of the actual written contributions that appear in this book were independently constructed. However, we have greatly influenced each other in these constructions through reading each other's published works, by arranging to work together from time to time, by exchanging ideas through correspondence, and by conducting joint workshops. I'm sure the reader will notice many regularities upon comparing the means that David and I employ and will appreciate the extent to which the association has been enriching to both of us.

Michael White

*Narrative Means to
Therapeutic Ends*

1. Story, Knowledge, and Power

In this chapter, I (M. W.) have presented an overview of some of the more recent developments in social theory that David and I have found of compelling interest, and some of what we believe to be the implications of those ideas for therapy. The discussion of theory includes some of Michel Foucault's thought on power and knowledge. Michel Foucault was a French intellectual who described himself as an "historian of systems of thought," and we believe his work to be of great importance.

Readers may be familiar with the debate about power that has surfaced in family therapy literature in recent years. Let me here take the risk of simplifying the positions enacted in this debate. To summarize: Some have argued that power doesn't really exist, but that it is something constructed in language and that those who experience its effects have participated in "bringing it forth." The other position is that power really exists and is wielded by some in order to oppress others. It seems that the terms of this debate have provided for an impasse, and this has not much advanced our thinking about power and its operation.

We believe that Foucault provides a way out of this impasse. However, those who are unfamiliar with his ideas and writing style often find him difficult to read. Here, I have done my best to present some of his ideas in a way that I hope makes them reasonably accessible. I'm not sure how successful I have been—this can only be determined by you, the reader.

Some readers might find it preferable to skip this chapter, go immediately to chapters 2, 3 and 4, and then return to the first chapter at a later stage when they are looking for answers to questions about the theoretical and political context of our working methods.

It was through the writings of Bateson (1972, 1979) that I was introduced to the "interpretive method." Here I am not referring to an interpretative method in the psychoanalytic sense. Social scientists refer to the interpretive method when they are studying the processes by which we make sense out of the world. Since we cannot know objective reality, all knowing requires an act of interpretation.

In challenging the appropriateness of linear notions of causality (principally derived from Newtonian physics) for the explanation of events in "living systems," Bateson argued that it was not possible for us to have an appreciation of objective reality. Referring to Korzybski's maxim, "the map is not the territory," he proposed that the understanding we have of, or the meaning we ascribe to, any event is determined and restrained by the receiving context for the event, that is, by the network of premises and presuppositions that constitute our maps of the world. Likening these maps to patterns, he argued that the interpretation of any events was determined by how it fit with known patterns of events, and he called this "part for whole coding" (Bateson, 1972). Not only, he argued, is the interpretation of an event determined by its receiving context but those events that cannot be "patterned" are not selected for survival; such events will not exist for us as facts.

Bateson's work also drew my attention to the importance of a much neglected dimension in therapy generally—the temporal dimension. In arguing that all information is necessarily "news of difference," and that it is the perception of difference that triggers all new responses in living systems, he demonstrated how the mapping of events through *time* is essential for the perception of difference, for the detection of change.

> Human sense organs can receive *only* news of difference, and the differences must be coded into events in *time* (i.e., into *changes*) in order to be perceptible. (Bateson, 1979, p. 79)

In considering the text analogy, I perceived a family resemblance of ideas between the notion of map and the notion of narrative. However, the notion of narrative, in that it requires the location of events in cross-time patterns, clearly has some advantage over the notion of map. Narrative incorporates the temporal dimension. To quote from Edward Bruner:

> I conclude by noting that narrative structure has an advantage over such related concepts as a metaphor or paradigm in that narrative emphasizes order and sequence, in a formal sense, and is more appropriate for the study of change, the life cycle, or any developmental process. Story as a model has a remarkable dual aspect — it is both linear and instantaneous. (1986a, p. 153)

In regard to family therapy — which has been our area of special interest — the interpretive method, rather than proposing that some underlying structure or dysfunction in the family determines the behavior and interactions of family members, would propose that it is the meaning that members attribute to events that determines their behavior. Thus, for some considerable time I have been interested in how persons organize their lives around specific meanings and how, in so doing, they inadvertently contribute to the "survival" of, as well as the "career" of, the problem. And, in contrast to some family therapy theorists, rather than considering the problem as being required in any way by persons or by the "system," I have been interested in the requirements of the problem for its survival and in the effect of those requirements on the lives and relationships of persons. I have proposed that the family members' cooperative but inadvertent responses to the problem's requirements, taken together, constitute the problem's life support system (White, 1986a).

In earlier publications I have referred to the way that problems can be situated within the context of "trends," thus appearing to have a life of their own in which they become more influential over time, and to how family members seem oblivious to the progressive and directional nature of their co-evolution around problem definitions; further, I have proposed the externalization of the problem as a mechanism for assisting family members to separate from "problem-saturated" descriptions of their lives and relationships (White, 1984, 1986a, 1986b, 1986c, 1987).*

The text analogy provided, for me, a second description of the way in which persons organize their lives around particular problems. Through the lens of this analogy, this organization can be considered to reflect the interaction of "readers" and "writers" around particular stories or narratives. The career or lifestyle of the problem becomes the story of the problem. This description opened up new areas of inquiry, including an exploration of those mechanisms that render particular texts meritorious in a literary sense, and encouraged me to propose a "therapy of literary merit" (White, 1988).

ANALOGY

At the outset of the social sciences, social scientists, in an effort to justify their endeavor, to establish plausibility, and to lay claim to legitimacy, turned to the positivist physical sciences for maps upon which to base their efforts in the interpretation of events in social systems. When positivism—the idea that it is possible to have direct knowledge of the world—was successfully challenged, and when social scientists realized that other scientists proceeded by analogy, and that the analogies they were appropriating had already been appropriated from elsewhere by the physical sciences—that "Science owes more to the steam engine than the steam engine owes to science" (Geertz, 1983, p. 22)—they were free to turn elsewhere in their search for metaphors from which to derive and elaborate theories. Geertz provides an account of this shift as the "refiguration of social thought."

> It has thus dawned on social scientists that they did not need to be mimic physicists or closet humanists or to invent some new realm of being to serve as the object of their investigations. Instead they could proceed with

*For a comprehensive summary of these ideas, see Munro (1987).

their vocation, trying to discover order in collective life.
. . . (1983, p. 21)

It is now widely accepted that any statement that postulates meaning is interpretive — that these statements are the outcome of an inquiry that is determined by our maps or analogies or, as Goffman (1974) puts it, "our interpretive frameworks." Thus, the analogies that we employ determine our examination of the world: the questions we ask about events, the realities we construct, and the "real" effects experienced by those parties to the inquiry. The analogies that we use determine the very distinctions that we "pull out" from the world.

My Table of Analogies which is, to an extent, informed by Geertz's representation of the development of the social sciences, reflects an attempt to consider the constructions that accompany some of the analogies taken up by the social sciences in its relatively short history. The analogy is specified in the first column, the way that the analogy constructs social organization in the second, the likely interpretation of events presented as problematic in the third, and in the fourth, the characteristic solutions to problematic events generated by the specified analogy. This table does not, by any means, present all the analogies that have been employed in the history of the social sciences.

How do we select or determine the analogies that we embrace? Our preferences for some analogies over others are multidetermined, including by ideological factors and by prevailing cultural practices. In privileging one analogy over another, we cannot resort to criteria such as correctness or accuracy, since such attributes cannot be established for any analogy. However, we can, at least to an extent, investigate the analogies through which we live by situating our own practices within the history of social thought and by examining and critiquing the effects of these practices.

The significance of the distinctions around different analogies, as made in the table, and the effects of the interpretations arrived at through recourse to these analogies can be illustrated in a couple of examples. Although these examples are both general and hypothetical, they do closely approximate actual circumstances and practices that we have witnessed.

TABLE OF ANALOGIES

ANALOGIES DRAWN FROM:	SOCIAL ORGANIZATION CONSTRUCTED AS:	PROBLEMS CONSTRUCTED AS:	SOLUTION CONSTRUCTED IN TERMS OF:
1. Positivist physical sciences	Elaborate machine, constituted by mechanics and hydraulics	Breakdown, reversal, insufficiency, damage	Isolating cause, precise analysis, repair, reconstruct, correct
2. Biological sciences	Quasi-organism	Symptomatic of underlying problem, serving a function, having utility	Identifying pathology, correct diagnosis, operating and excising pathology
3. Social Sciences			
3(a) Game theory	Serious game	Strategies, moves	Contest, countermoves, strategizing
3(b) Drama	Living room drama	Roles, scripts, performances	Revising roles, selecting alternative dramatic form
3(c) Ritual process	Rite of passage	Transition — separation, betwixt and between, re-incorporation.	Mapping, drawing distinctions around status 1 and status 2
3(d) Text	Behavioral text	Performance of oppressive, dominant story or knowledge	Opening space for the authoring of alternative stories

Example 1

If a person experiencing some form of acute crisis presents to a "clinic," and if the work of this clinic is oriented by analogies drawn from the tradition of positivist science, then it is likely that the crisis will be interpreted as some sort of breakdown and regression. Attempts will be made to convert the person's experience into a precise diagnosis according to some system of classification, and questions will be introduced that attempt to identify a cause of the "breakdown" that is consistent with the model. Then various procedures will be performed by experts — procedures that include the tracing of the history of the damage and that revise the past according to the tenets of the model. The goal would be to retrieve and reconstruct the person, thereby returning him or her to a "good enough" level of functioning.

If, however, that class of ritual process called a "rite of passage" (van Gennep, 1960; Turner, 1969)* provides the receiving context for the very same crisis, then a different construction of the problem will be invited and different questions will be asked. The crisis will be interpreted as relating to some aspect of a transition or rite of passage in the person's life, and questions will be introduced that locate the crisis in relation to:

1. The separation phase — perhaps from some status, aspect of identity, or role that is determined to be no longer viable for the person concerned;
2. The liminal or betwixt and between phase — characterized by some discomfort, confusion, disorganization, and perhaps heightened expectations for the future; and
3. The reincorporation phase — characterized by the arrival at some new status that specifies new responsibilities and privileges for the person concerned.

---

*David Epston has popularized this analogy in Australia and New Zealand. With his encouragement, it has been taken up by others and applied in a wide range of contexts. For an excellent discussion of the application of this analogy in residential care contexts, see Menses and Durrant (1986).

Thus, the rite of passage analogy could orient questions that invite persons to determine (a) what the crisis might be telling them about what they could be separating from that was not viable for them—perhaps certain negative attitudes that they have towards themselves or that others have towards them, or expectations and prescriptions for their life and relationships that they experience as impoverishing; (b) what clues the crisis gives about the new status and roles that could become available to them; and (c) when, how, and under what circumstances these new roles and status might be realized. Thus, a receiving context established by this rite of passage analogy can construct the crisis within terms of progress rather than regression, without denying its distressing aspects.

Example 2

At times, couples present for therapy with certain problems after an initial phase in their relationship that was relatively enjoyable, one that the partners found mutually satisfying. If the receiving context for this presentation is informed by analogies from the biological sciences, then the initial nonproblematic phase of the relationship may be assigned the mantle of a "honeymoon phase," and thus denigrated as an inaccurate reflection of the relationship, while the second, problematic phase will be assumed to be a true reflection of the state of affairs in the relationship, one that was always present and lurking at a level beneath the surface—a state of affairs that was misrepresented and glossed over by the honeymoon phase of the relationship. These problems, in turn, can then be considered to reflect still deeper processes of dysfunction and associated psychopathology, deeper processes that are ascribed an objective reality or "truth" status. Experts will institute operations to identify these deeper levels of objective reality, tracing the history of the dysfunction and psychopathology, perhaps down through the families of origins of both parties and into the relationships of their respective parents. This is a typical construction of the form of depth psychology that so saturates western culture.

If, however, the text analogy provides the receiving context for the couple's experiences, then what the biological model constitutes as levels can be turned through 90°, stood on their ends, to be considered alternative and competing stories. The story that the couple finds most attractive can then be identified. Under these circumstances, this is invariably the story of the first, non-problematic phase. This first story can then be examined for what it might tell the spouses about their problem-solving ability, and the history of this ability can be traced into their families of origins. Plans can then be made by the couple to replicate, re-perform, and extend these skills at difficult times in their relationship.

THE TEXT ANALOGY

We have a strong preference for those analogies on the lower part of the table, those that relate to the more recent develop-ments in the social sciences and do not propose objective realities. In the present discussion, attention will be given to the text analo-gy, one that has provided what Geertz refers to as the "broadest and most recent refiguration of social thought."

Social scientists became interested in the text analogy following observations that, although a piece of behavior occurs in time in such a way that it no longer exists in the present by the time it is attended to, the meaning that is ascribed to the behavior survives across time. It was this ascription of meaning that drew their atten-tion, and in their attempts to understand this they began to invoke the text analogy. This enabled the interaction of persons to be considered as the interaction of readers around particular texts. This analogy also made it possible to conceive of the evolution of lives and relationships in terms of the reading and writing of texts, insofar as every new reading of a text is a new interpretation of it, and thus a different writing of it.

Concluding that we cannot have direct knowledge of the world, social scientists proposed that what persons know of life they know through "lived experience." This proposal led to the generation of new questions: How do persons organize their stock of lived expe-rience? What do persons do with this experience in order to give it meaning and to make sense out of their lives? How is lived experi-ence given expression? Those social scientists embracing the text analogy responded by arguing that, in order to make sense of our lives and to express ourselves, experience must be "storied" and it is this storying that determines the meaning ascribed to experience.

In striving to make sense of life, persons face the task of arranging their experiences of events in sequences across time in such a way as to arrive at a coherent account of themselves and the world around them. Specific experiences of events of the past and present, and those that are predicted to occur in the future, must be connected in a lineal sequence to develop this account. This account can be referred to as a story or self-narrative (see Gergen & Gergen, 1984). The success of this storying of experience provides persons with a sense of continuity and meaning in their lives, and this is relied upon for the ordering of daily lives and for the interpretation of further experiences. Since all stories have a beginning (or a history), a middle (or a present), and an ending (or a future), then the interpretation of current events is as much future-shaped as it is past-determined. To illustrate this point, I will refer to some of Edward Bruner's (1986a) field work with Native North Americans.

In discussing his study of the ethnographic stories of the Native North American, Bruner demonstrates how the interpretation of their current living circumstances shifted radically with the generation of a new story that proposed an alternative history and future. In the 1930s and 1940s, the dominant story about the Native North American constructed the past as glorious and the future as assimilation. In attributing meaning to current circumstances within the context of this story, anthropologists and Native North Americans alike interpreted the "facts" of the daily lives of the Native North Americans as reflective of breakdown and disorganization, as a transitional state along the route from glory to assimilation. This interpretation had real effects. For example, it justified certain interventions of the dominant culture, including those relating to the appropriation of territories.

In the 1950s there emerged a new story, one that constructed the past as exploitation and the future as resurgence. Although it could be assumed that the "facts" of the daily existence of the Native North American did not significantly change through this period, with this new story providing the receiving context, a new interpretation of these facts arose.* They were now considered to reflect not disorganization, but resistance. This new interpretation also had its real effects, including the development of a movement that confronted the dominant culture with the issue of land rights. Bruner concludes:

> In my view, we began with a narrative that already contains a beginning and an ending, which frame and hence enables us to interpret the present. It is not that we initially have a body of data, the facts, and we then must construct a story or theory to account for them. Instead . . . the narrative structures we construct are not secondary narratives about data but primary narratives that establish what is to count as data. New narratives yield new vocabulary, syntax, and meaning in our ethnographic accounts; they define what constitute the data of those accounts. (1986a, p. 143)

It is clear that the sense of meaning and continuity that is achieved through the storying of experience is gained at a price. A narrative can never encompass the full richness of our lived experience:

> . . . life experience is richer than discourse. Narrative structures organize and give meaning to experience, but there are always feelings and lived experience not fully encompassed by the dominant story. (E. Bruner, 1986a, p. 143)

The structuring of a narrative requires recourse to a selective process in which we prune, from our experience, those events that do not fit with the dominant evolving stories that we and others have

---

*Apart from allowing for a reinterpretation of these facts, the second story also enabled Native North Americans to perform meaning around and express many aspects of their lived experience that were not visible in "readings" of the first story.

about us. Thus, over time and of necessity, much of our stock of lived experience goes unstoried and is never "told" or expressed. It remains amorphous, without organization and without shape:

> Some experiences are inchoate, in that we simply do not understand what we are experiencing, either because the experiences are not storyable, or because we lack the performative and narrative resources, or because vocabulary is lacking. (E. Bruner, 1986b, pp. 6–7)

If we accept that persons organize and give meaning to their experience through the storying of experience, and that in the performance of these stories they express selected aspects of their lived experience, then it follows that these stories are constitutive — shaping lives and relationships:

> It is in the performance of an expression that we re-experience, re-live, re-create, re-tell, re-construct, and re-fashion our culture. The performance does not release a pre-existing meaning that lies dormant in the text.... Rather the performance itself is constitutive. (E. Bruner, 1986b, p. 11)

From this it can be seen that the text analogy advances the idea that the stories or narratives that persons live through determine their interaction and organization, and that the evolution of lives and relationships occurs through the performance of such stories or narratives. Thus, the text analogy is distinct from those analogies that would propose an underlying structure or pathology in families and persons that is constitutive or shaping of their lives and relationships.

The evolution of lives and relationships through the performance of stories relates to the "relative indeterminancy" of all texts. The presence of implicit meaning, of the varying perspectives of the different "readers" of particular events, and of a diverse range of metaphors available for the description of such events consigns a degree of ambiguity to every text. And, in Iser's (1978) sense, this ambiguity or indeterminacy requires persons to engage in "performances of meaning under the guidance of the text." In studying texts of literary merit, Jerome Bruner states:

> It is this "relative indeterminancy of a text" that "allows a spectrum of actualizations." And so, "literary texts initiate 'performances' of meaning rather than actually formulating meaning themselves." (J. Bruner, 1986, p. 25)

For Geertz, the indeterminancy of texts and the constitutive aspect of the performance of texts provide good cause to celebrate:

> The wrenching question, sour and disabused, that Lionel Trilling somewhere quotes an eighteenth-century aesthetician as asking—"How Comes It that we all start out Originals and end up Copies?"—finds ... an answer that is surprisingly reassuring: it is the copying that originates. (1986, p. 380)

Stories are full of gaps which persons must fill in order for the story to be performed. These gaps recruit the lived experience and the imagination of persons. With every performance, persons are reauthoring their lives. The evolution of lives is akin to the process of reauthoring, the process of persons' entering into stories, taking them over and making them their own.

Thus, in two senses, the text analogy introduces us to an intertextual world. In the first sense, it proposes that persons' lives are situated in texts within texts. In the second sense, every telling or retelling of a story, through its performance, is a new telling that encapsulates, and expands upon the previous telling.

THE TEXT ANALOGY AND THERAPY

We have considered the proposal that persons give meaning to their lives and relationships by storying their experience and that, in interacting with others in the performance of these stories, they are active in the shaping of their lives and relationships. If we accept this proposal, what then do we make of a person's experience of problems and the presentation of these for therapy?*

There are a number of possible assumptions that could be made about this. We could assume that the person's experience is problematic to him because he is being situated in stories that others have about him and his relationships, and that these stories are dominant to the extent that they allow insufficient space for the performance of the person's preferred stories. Or we could assume that the person is actively participating in the performance of stories that she finds unhelpful, unsatisfying, and dead-ended, and that these stories do not sufficiently encapsulate the person's lived experience or are very significantly contradicted by important aspects of the person's lived experience.

Doubtless, many other assumptions could be explored. For example, we could assume that the experience of particular problems and the presentation of these in therapy is part of the performance of a story that has become popular in western society in recent years. However, for the purposes of this present discussion, we make the general assumption that persons experience problems, for which they frequently seek therapy, when the narratives in which they are "storying" their experience, and/or in which they are having their experience "storied" by others, do not sufficiently represent their lived experience, and that, in these circumstances,

---

*We believe that "therapy" as a term is inadequate to describe the work discussed here. The *Penguin Macquarie Dictionary* describes therapy as the "treatment of disease, disorder, defect, etc., as by some remedial or curative process." In our work we do not construct problems in terms of disease and do not imagine that we do anything that relates to "a cure."

There have recently been some attempts, in the literature, to address concerns of this nature, and the notion of "therapeutic conversations" has been proposed (e.g., Anderson & Goolishian, 1988). This description does have appeal, perhaps because, in part, the terms "therapy" and "conversation" are contradictory by definition, and "conversation" goes some way towards challenging the realities constructed by, and the mystification introduced by, the term "therapy." However, we are not entirely satisfied that the term conversation is sufficient as a description of an approach to the re-storying of experience, or that this term adequately represents the unique process we describe.

there will be significant aspects of their lived experience that contradict these dominant narratives.

What are the implications of these assumptions for that activity we call therapy? If we accept the assumptions made above as reasonable, then we could also assume that, when persons seek therapy, an acceptable outcome would be the identification or generation of alternative stories that enable them to perform new meanings, bringing with them desired possibilities — new meanings that persons will experience as more helpful, satisfying, and open-ended.

Lived Experience and Alternative Stories

A case has been made for the notions that persons are rich in lived experience, that only a fraction of this experience can be storied and expressed at any one time, and that a great deal of lived experience inevitably falls outside the dominant stories about the lives and relationships of persons. Those aspects of lived experience that fall outside of the dominant story provide a rich and fertile source for the generation, or re-generation, of alternative stories.

Following Goffman (1961), I have referred to these aspects of lived experience that fall outside the dominant story as "unique outcomes." In defining unique outcomes, he states that in the structuring of experience into "any social strand of any person's course through life . . . unique outcomes are neglected in favor of such changes over time as are basic and common to the members of a social category although occurring independently to each of them" (p. 127).* Goffman's notions of a "social strand" and "social category" can be likened to the notion of "dominant story" and the group of persons of a specified identity whose lives are situated in this story.

---

*For me, this idea has an identity with Bateson's notion of the stochastic process: "If a sequence of events combines a random component with a selective process, so that only certain outcomes of the random are allowed to endure, that sequence is said to be stochastic" (1979, p. 253).

Although the existence of these unique outcomes can never be predicted by a reading of the "social strand" or the dominant story of a person's life, they are always present. They include the whole gamut of events, feelings, intentions, thoughts, actions, etc., that have a historical, present, or future location and that cannot be accommodated by the dominant story. The identification of unique outcomes can be facilitated by the externalization of the dominant "problem-saturated" description or story of a person's life and relationships. The externalization of the problem-saturated story can be initiated by encouraging the externalization of the problem, and then by the mapping of the problem's influence in the person's life and relationships. This is begun by asking persons about how *the problem* has been affecting their lives and their relationships. By achieving this separation from the problem-saturated description of life, from this habitual reading of the dominant story, persons are more able to identify unique outcomes.

This externalization is also helpful in the interruption of the habitual reading and performance of these stories. As persons become separated from their stories, they are able to experience a sense of personal agency; as they break from their performance of their stories, they experience a capacity to intervene in their own lives and relationships. The discovery of unique outcomes, as well as the externalizing of the problem, can then be further assisted by encouraging persons to map their influence, and the influence of their relationships with others, on the "life" of the problem. This approach is discussed in detail in Chapter 2 and elsewhere (White, 1986a, 1988).

When unique outcomes are identified, persons can be invited to ascribe meaning to them. Success in this ascription of meaning requires that the unique outcomes be plotted into an alternative story or narrative. And in this process, as acknowledged by Victor Turner (1986), "imagining" plays a very significant role. Various questions can be introduced that assist in engaging persons in this ascription of new meaning, questions that actively involve them in, as Myerhoff (1982) would put it, the "re-authoring" of their lives and their relationships. These questions can include those that invite persons to account for the unique outcomes (for example, "How did you manage to resist the influence of the problem on this occasion?"), those that invite a redescription of self, others, and relationships according to what is reflected in the unique outcomes (for example, "What does your success at resisting the problem say about you as a person?"), and those that invite persons to speculate about some of the new possibilities that might accompany the unique outcomes (for example, "What difference will this news about yourself make to your next stop?").* In considering therapy as a context for the re-authoring of lives and relationships, I have proposed a "therapy of literary merit" (White, 1988).

As alternative stories become available to be performed, other "sympathetic" and previously neglected aspects of the person's experience can be expressed and circulated. Inviting persons to be an audience to their own performance of these alternative stories enhances the survival of the stories and the sense of personal agency. This can be facilitated by encouraging persons to identify those expressions of aspects of lived experience that would have previously gone unstoried and to review the real effects of these expressions in their lives and relationships.

The endurance of new stories, as well as their elaboration, can also be enhanced by recruiting an "external" audience. There is a dual aspect to this enhancement. Firstly, in the act of witnessing the performance of a new story, the audience contributes to the writing of new meanings; this has real effects on the audience's interaction with the story's subject. Secondly, when the subject of the story "reads" the audience's experience of the new performance, either through speculation about these experiences or by a more direct identification, he or she engages in revisions and extensions of the new story.

As discussed, in a therapy of oral tradition, the re-authoring of lives and relationships is achieved primarily, although not exclusively, through a process of questioning. In a therapy that incorporates the narrative tradition, this is also achieved through recourse to a variety of documents. Various forms of such documents are presented later in this book.

In conclusion, the re-storying of experience necessitates the

---

*For further examples of such questions, see White (1988).

active involvement of persons in the reorganization of their experience, "in the free recombination of the factors of culture into any and every possible pattern" (Turner, 1974, p. 255). This, along with invitations for persons to engage in activities that generate an awareness of a process in which they are simultaneously performers in and audience to their own performance, and a consciousness of one's production of one's productions, provides for a context of reflexivity (see Tomm, 1987). This context brings forth new choices for persons regarding the authoring of themselves, others, and their relationships.

DOMINANT NARRATIVE AS DOMINANT KNOWLEDGE AND UNIT OF POWER

One helpful aspect of the text analogy is that it assists us to consider the stories that provide the broader sociopolitical context of the person's experience. The first story about the Native North Americans was framed by a dominant ideology of its time in the United States, one that invoked the melting-pot dream of "one America." The second story was framed by different ideals, those that related to the emerging acknowledgment of muticulturalism and the identification and appreciation of *many* Americas. Of course, the extent to which this second story has prevailed is debatable.

Just as the stories of the Native American are framed by a broader context, so are the stories of persons who come for therapy. While the text analogy provides a frame that enables us to consider the broader sociopolitical context of persons whose lives are situated in many texts, it also enables us to include a consideration of *power* in its operation and effects on lives and relationships. This possibility is an important one, as the vista of power has been much overlooked in the therapy literature generally, and especially in the benign view that we frequently take of our own practices.

Those analyses of power that have appeared in the therapy literature have traditionally represented it in individual terms, such as a biological phenomenon that affects the individual psyche or as individual pathology that is the inevitable outcome of early traumatic personal experiences, or in Marxist terms as a class phenomenon. More recently, feminist analyses of power have framed it as a gender-specific repressive phenomenon. This has sensitized many therapists to the gender-related experiences of abuse, exploitation, and oppression.

Although we have witnessed the liberating effects of the feminist analysis of power as a gender-specific and repressive mechanism, we believe it important to consider the more general spectrum of power as well—not only its repressive aspects but also its constitutive aspects. To this end, the work of Michel Foucault is of importance. The following discussion of Foucault's contribution to the analysis of power is not by any means exhaustive; just some of his concepts are presented. Moreover, readers will notice a certain inevitable overlapping of ideas under the different headings.

Knowledge and Power as Constitutive

Commonly, it is proposed that power is repressive in its operations and in its effects, that it is negative in force and character. Power is said to disqualify, limit, deny, and contain. However, Foucault argues that we predominantly experience the positive or constitutive effects of power, that we are subject to power through normalizing "truths" that shape our lives and relationships. These "truths", in turn, are constructed or produced in the operation of power (Foucault, 1979, 1980, 1984a).

Thus, when discussing the positive effects of power, Foucault is not making reference to "positive" in the usual sense, that is, as something desirable or beneficial. Rather, he is referring to it in the sense that power is constitutive or shaping of persons' lives. The notion of a power that is negative in its effects contributes a theory of repression, while the notion of a power that is positive in its effects leads to a theory about its role in "making up" persons' lives. And when discussing "truths," Foucault is subscribing not to the belief that there exist objective or intrinsic facts about the nature of persons but instead to constructed ideas that are accorded a truth status. These "truths" are "normalizing" in the sense that they construct norms around which persons are incited to shape or constitute their lives. Therefore, these are "truths" that actually specify persons' lives.

According to Foucault, a primary effect of this power through "truth" and "truth" through power is the specification of a form of individuality, an individuality that is, in turn, a "vehicle" of power. Rather than proposing that this form of power represses, Foucault argues that it subjugates. It forges persons as "docile bodies" and conscripts them into activities that support the proliferation of "global" and "unitary" knowledges, as well as the techniques of power. However, in referring to "global" and "unitary" knowledges, Foucault is not proposing that there are knowledges that are universally accepted. Rather, he is referring to those knowledges that make unitary and global truth claims — the "objective reality" knowledges of the modern scientific disciplines. As subjects of this power, through knowledge, we are:

> . . . judged, condemned, classified, determined in our un-
> dertaking, destined to a certain mode of living or dying, as
> a function of the true discourses which are the bearers of
> the specific effects of power. (1980, p. 94)

The constitutive effects of power through normalizing truths can be illustrated through a discussion of Foucault's (1984a) account of the history of sexual desire. In tracing the history of sexuality, he challenges the popular wisdom that, throughout the Victorian regime, sex and power were linked through the relation of repression. Instead, he argues that this era saw a proliferation of discourses that relate to sex and an increasing "incitement" for persons to talk about it. In tracing the details of this "great sexual sermon," he sketched changes in confessional practices through the 17th century and developments in the forms to control the sexuality of children.

The emphasis in confessional practices shifted to incorporate not just acts, but all of those thoughts, feelings, fantasies, dreams, etc., that could possibly have even the most slender relation to sexual desire. For the detection of all possibilities, methods were introduced for the surveillance of the words that one used and of the movements of one's body. Procedures were also developed for listening to all utterances of sexual desire and for recording and distributing the various observations and findings of these activities. In short, this era saw the transformation of desire into discourse, along with the construction of a normative "truth" about sexuality.

In regard to the "dangerous" sexuality of children, there emerged a whole field of expert opinion that was devoted to its articulation and regulation. Numerous manuals appeared that encouraged, in parents and other guardians, a preoccupation with the sexual development of children and with the many possible complications in this development; these manuals provided meticulous instruction on the correct methods for the supervision of childhood sexuality:

> Around the schoolboy and his sex there proliferated a whole literature of precepts, opinions, observations, medical advice, clinical cases, outlines for reform, and plans for ideal institutions. (1984a, p. 28)

Thus, according to Foucault, the notions of a historical sexual repression and a modern sexual liberation are "ruses" that disguise what has actually taken place — that is, an incitement to discourse about sexual desire, the construction of knowledge about sexuality, and the specification of forms of sexuality according to these "truths." The lives of persons are constituted through these specifications and through the techniques for the ongoing production and proliferation of "truth" discourses on sexual desire:

> What is peculiar to the modern societies, in fact, is not that they consigned sex to a shadow existence, but that they dedicated themselves to speaking of it *ad infinitum*, while exploiting it as *the* secret. (1984a, p. 35)

Power/Knowledge

In considering the constitutive dimension of power, Foucault concludes that power and knowledge are inseparable — so much so that he prefers to place the terms together as power/knowledge or knowledge/power. In studying the history of systems of thought, he concludes that the emergence and spectacular success of the "disciplines" of life, labor, and language from the 17th century on was dependent on the techniques of power, and that, in turn, the expansionist quality of modern power was dependent upon progress in the construction of these knowledges that propose the "truth." Thus, it can be seen that a domain of knowledge is a domain of power, and a domain of power is a domain of knowledge:

> There can be no possible exercise of power without a certain economy of discourses of truth which operates through and on the basis of this association. We are subjected to the production of truth through power and we cannot exercise power except through the production of truth. (1980, p. 93)

In putting power and knowledge together in this way, Foucault blocks a formulation of power and knowledge that would suggest knowledge only becomes problematic when it is wielded by those in power to suit their own ends. Instead, he argues that, mostly, we are all acting coherently within and through a given field of power/knowledge, and that, although these actions have their very real effects, they cannot be identified with special motives. Here Foucault is not talking about all forms of power, but about a particularly modern and insidious form of power.

Foucault thus dissuades us from a concern with an "internal point of view" for the explanation of the operation of power, challenging any preoccupations we might have with who intends its effects and what decisions are made about its exercise. Since we are all caught up in a net or web of power/knowledge, it is not possible to act apart from this domain, and we are simultaneously undergoing the effects of power and exercising this power in relation to others. However, this does not, by any means, suggest that all persons are equal in the exercise of power, nor that some do not suffer its subjugating effects very much more than others.

Let us not, therefore, ask why certain people want to dominate, what they seek, what is their overall strategy. Let us ask, instead, how things work at the level of ongoing subjugation, at the level of those continuous and uninterrupted processes which subject our bodies, govern our gestures, dictate our behaviours, etc. In other words . . . we should try to discover how it is that subjects are gradually, progressively, really and materially constituted through a multiplicity of organisms, forces, energies, materials, desires, thoughts, etc. We should try to grasp subjection in its material instance as a constitution of subjects. (1980, p. 97)

Foucault's conception of the inseparability of power/knowledge is reflected in his confrontation of those who argue for the ascendancy of particular knowledges over others. He would ask: What alternative knowledges would they disqualify and what persons or groups of persons are likely to be diminished through the success of such arguments for ascendancy?

Foucault maintains that it is the isolation of specific knowledges from the discontinuous knowledges that circulate around them that invests their discourses with the effect of power. This isolation is essentially achieved by the development of "objective reality" discourses that qualify these knowledges for a place in the hierarchy of scientific knowledges. Foucault traced the history of these knowledges that were accorded this status, investigating their effects, their limitations and their dangers.

The central issue of philosophy and critical thought since the eighteenth century has always been . . . What is this reason that we use? What are its historical effects? What are its limits and what are its dangers? (1984b, p. 249)

Ascending vs. Descending Analysis of Power

Foucault argues for an ascending analysis of power, not a descending analysis. Rather than proposing that the techniques of power are put into operation from above to transform those below, he proposes that the origination of these techniques occurs at the local level. In fact, their ready availability was a precondition for the success of the growth of unitary and global knowledges from the 17th century on, as well as for the rise of capitalism.

These techniques were essentially the techniques of social control, "of subjugation," techniques for the "objectification" or "thingification" of persons, and for the objectification of the bodies of persons. They included techniques for the organization and arrangement of persons in space in ways that allowed for the greatest efficiency and economy; those for the registration and classification of persons; those for the exclusion of groups of persons and for the ascription of identity to these groups; techniques for the isolation of persons and for the effective means of observation (surveillance) and evaluation.

Foucault also detailed the technology that became available to recruit persons into an active role in their own subjugation. When conditions are established for persons to experience ongoing evaluation according to particular institutionalized "norms," when these conditions cannot be escaped, and when persons can be isolated in their experience of such conditions, then they will become the guardians of themselves. In these circumstances, persons will perpetually evaluate their own behavior and engage in operations on themselves to forge themselves as "docile bodies."* According to Foucault, we live in a society where evaluation or normalizing judgment has replaced the judiciary and torture as a primary mechanism of social control: This is a society of the everpresent "gaze."**

---

*Anorexia nervosa and bulimia may well reflect the pinnacle of achievement of this form of power.
**According to Foucault (1979), Jeremy Bentham's Panopticon was proposed as an ideal model for this form of social control. This model is discussed more explicitly in Chapter 2. It can be argued that, in the relationships between the sexes, this model is gender biased, with men more often the instruments of the normalizing gaze and women more often its subject.

Thus, Foucault is concerned with more than ideology and its effects. He is concerned with the very techniques of power that are required for the growth of knowledge:

> It is both much more and much less than ideology. It is the production of effective instruments for the formation and accumulation of knowledge — methods of observation, techniques of registration, procedures for investigation and research, apparatuses of control. All this means that power, when it is exercised through these subtle mechanisms, cannot but evolve, organize and put into circulation a knowledge, or rather apparatuses of knowledge, which are not ideological constructs. (1980, p. 102)

Foucault also argues that just as these techniques were developed at the local level, it is at this level that the exercise of power is the least concealed and thus most available to critique. He encourages the study of the history of power and its effects at the "extremities" of society, such as in clinics, local organizations, the family, etc.

Subjugated Knowledges

Foucault not only provides an analysis of the "global totalitarian" theories but also reviews those other knowledges — the "subjugated knowledges." He proposes two classes of subjugated knowledges. One class is constituted by those previously established or "erudite" knowledges that have been written out of the record by the revision of history achieved through the ascendance of a more global and unitary knowledge. According to Foucault, these erudite knowledges have been buried, hidden, and disguised "in a functional coherence of formal systematizations" that is designed to "mask the ruptural effects of conflict and struggle." These knowledges can be resurrected only by careful and meticulous scholarship, and in this resurrection, the history of struggle again becomes visible and unitary truth claims challenged.*

The second class of subjugated knowledges are those which Foucault refers to as "local popular" or "indigenous" knowledges: those "regional" knowledges that are currently in circulation but are denied or deprived of the space in which they could be adequately performed. These are knowledges that survive only at the margins of society and are lowly ranked—considered insufficient and exiled from the legitimate domain of the formal knowledges and the accepted sciences. They are the "naive knowledges, located low down on the hierarchy, beneath the required level of cognition or scientificity" (Foucault, 1980).

Foucault suggests that, through the recovery of the details of these autonomous and disqualified knowledges (in the "union of erudite knowledge and local memories"), we can rediscover the history of struggle and conflict. And, in the provision of an adequate space in which these knowledges can be performed, we can develop an effective criticism of the dominant knowledges, a criticism "whose validity is not dependent on the approval of the established regimes of thought."

> I also believe that it is through the re-emergence of these low-ranking knowledges, these unqualified, even directly disqualified knowledges . . . and which involve what I would call a popular knowledge . . . that it is through the re-appearance of this knowledge, of these local popular knowledges, these disqualified knowledges, that criticism performs its work. (1980, p. 82)

Thus, it is clear that Foucault does not propose any alternative ideology, any other ideal unitary knowledge around which we can organize our lives. Neither does he suggest that it is possible to

---

*For an example of an attempt to resurrect subjugated erudite knowledge, see Dale Spender's *Women of Ideas: And What Men Have Done to Them* (1983).

"deny" knowledge, that is, to act apart from and experience the world from outside of the mediating effects of knowledge and discursive practices. Nor does he argue for a return to a version of positivism that attempts to establish practices that are based on the idea of "an immediate experience that escapes encapsulation in knowledge." Instead, he argues for the "insurrection" of the subjugated knowledges against the "institutions and against the effects of the knowledge and power that invests scientific discourse," for the insurrection of knowledges:

> ... that are opposed primarily not to the contents, methods or concepts of a science, but to the effects of the centralising powers which are linked to the institution and functioning of an organised scientific discourse within a society such as ours. (1980, p. 84)

ALTERNATIVE STORIES AND CULTURALLY AVAILABLE DISCOURSES

I have argued that the text analogy provides a frame that enables us to consider the broader sociopolitical context of persons' lives and relationships, and that Foucault's analysis of power/ knowledge can provide us with some details of that broader context. I have also provided a summary of some of Foucault's thought relating to power and knowledge. What are the practical implications of this for therapy?

In the foregoing discussion of the text analogy, it was proposed that meaning is derived through the structuring of experience into stories, and that the performance of these stories is constitutive of lives and relationships. As this storying of experience is dependent upon language, in accepting this premise we are also proposing that we ascribe meaning to our experience and constitute our lives and relationships through language. When engaging in language, we are not engaging in a neutral activity. There exists a stock of culturally available discourses that are considered appropriate and relevant to the expression or representation of particular aspects of experience. Thus, our understandings of our lived experience, including those that we refer to as "self-understandings," are mediated through language. And it can be expected that those "truth" discourses of the unitary and global knowledges contribute significantly in this mediation of understanding and in the constitution of personhood and of relationship.

How does this modify or contribute to our general assumption about a person's experience of a problem: that persons experience problems which they frequently present for therapy when the narratives in which they are storying their experience, and/or in which they are having their experience storied by others, do not sufficiently represent their lived experience, and that, in these circumstances, there will be significant aspects of their lived experience that contradict this dominant narrative? First, in the light of Foucault's analysis, we could further assume that those narratives that do not sufficiently represent a person's lived experiences or are contradicted by vital aspects of that experience are significantly informed by the "truth" discourses of the unitary knowledges. Second, we could assume that persons are incited to perform operations, through the techniques of power, on their lives and relationships in order to subject themselves and others to the specifications for personhood and relationship that are carried in these "truth" discourses.

Below I present some ideas regarding an orientation in therapy that is considerably informed by Foucault's thought. This will be followed by discussion of therapy practices based on the above-mentioned assumption about persons' experience of problems, as revised by Foucault's analysis of power/knowledge.

Orientation in Therapy

In accepting Foucault's analysis of the rise of global and unitary knowledges (that is, the objective reality scientific knowledges that make global and unitary truth claims), we become wary of situating our practices in those "truth" discourses of the professional disciplines, those discourses that propose and assert objective reality accounts of the human condition. And since it is the isolation of these knowledges from knowledges at large, as well as their establishment in the hierarchy of scientificity, that endows them with their power, we challenge the isolation of the knowledges of the professional disciplines from the field of discontinuous knowledges. In addition, we challenge the scientism of the human sciences.

If we accept that power and knowledge are inseparable — that a domain of knowledge is a domain of power and a domain of power is a domain of knowledge — and if we accept that we are simultaneously undergoing the effects of power and exercising power over others, then we are unable to take a benign view of our own practices. Nor are we able simply to assume that our practices are primarily determined by our motives, or that we can avoid all participation in the field of power/knowledge through an examination of such personal motives.

Instead, we would assume that we are always participating simultaneously in domains of power and knowledge. Thus, we would endeavor to establish conditions that encourage us to critique our own practices formed in this domain. We would work to identify the context of ideas in which our practices are situated and explore the history of these ideas. This would enable us to identify more readily the effects, dangers, and limitations of these ideas and of our own practices. And, instead of believing that therapy does not have anything to do with social control, we would assume that this was always a strong possibility. Thus, we would work to identify and critique those aspects of our work that might relate to the techniques of social control.

If we accept Foucault's proposal that the techniques of power that "incite" persons to constitute their lives through "truth" are developed and perfected at the local level and are then taken up at the broader levels, then, in joining with persons to challenge these practices, we also accept that we are inevitably engaged in a political activity. (We would also acknowledge that, if we do not join with persons to challenge these techniques of power, then we are also engaged in political activity.) This is not a political activity that involves the proposal of an alternative ideology, but one that challenges the techniques that subjugate persons to a dominant ideology.

Separating from the Unitary Knowledges

The externalization of the problem helps persons identify and separate from unitary knowledges and "truth" discourses that are subjugating of them. In mapping the influence of the problem in the person's life and relationships, these unitary knowledges can be exposed by encouraging persons to identify beliefs about themselves, others, and their relationships that are reinforced and confirmed by the continued presence of the problem. These beliefs usually relate to a sense of failure to achieve certain expectations, to replicate certain specifications, or to meet certain norms. These expectations, specifications, and norms can provide details about the "truths" of the unitary knowledges. The history of the effect of these "truths" in the constitution of the person's life and relationships can then be explored.

Through this process of externalization, persons gain a reflexive perspective on their lives, and new options become available to them in challenging the "truths" that they experience as defining and specifying of them and their relationships. This helps them refuse the objectification or "thingification" of themselves and their bodies through knowledge.

Challenging the Techniques of Power

As with the unitary knowledges, the techniques of power that "incite" persons to constitute their lives through "truth" can be successfully challenged through recourse to the externalization of the problem. As previously mentioned, these techniques include those for the organization of persons in space, those for the registration and classification of persons, those for the exclusion of groups of persons and for the ascription of identity to those groups, and those techniques for the isolation of persons and for the effective means of surveillance and evaluation.

As we explore the effects of the problem on the lives and relationships of persons, the requirements for the problem's survival can be identified. These requirements include specific arrangements of persons, as well as particular relationships to oneself and others, and can be identified through an exploration of the way that the problem appears to compel persons to treat themselves and others. Thus, one uncovers the details of the techniques of power that persons are being subjected to, subjecting themselves to, and subjecting others to.

Once these techniques have been identified, unique outcomes can be located through an investigation of those occasions when the person could have subjected himself or others to these techniques but refused to do so. The person can then be invited to engage in a performance of meaning around these unique outcomes. To this end, questions can be asked about how the person's defiance or refusal to perform according to the requirements of the problem might have helped him to undermine the problem and the ideas that it both reinforces and depends upon for its survival. Other examples of defiance can be identified and linked together to provide a historical account of resistance. Speculation can be invited about other opportunities that might be available to extend this account of resistance and the likely effects on the person's life and relationships should this be successful. In identifying these unique outcomes, subjugation to the techniques of "normalizing judgment"—the evaluation and classification of persons and relationships according to dominant "truths"—can be effectively challenged. "Docile bodies" become "enlivened spirits."

Resurrecting the Subjugated Knowledges

Insofar as the desirable outcome of therapy is the generation of alternative stories that incorporate vital and previously neglected aspects of lived experience, and insofar as these stories incorporate alternative knowledges, it can be argued that the identification of and provision of the space for the performance of these knowledges is a central focus of the therapeutic endeavor.

As we have seen, the externalization of the problem can be utilized en route to the identification and externalization of the unitary knowledge. This is helpful in that it assists persons in challenging the "truths" that specify their lives—to protest their subjugation to unitary knowledges. Also, in helping persons separate from these unitary knowledges, externalization opens space for the identification of and circulation of alternative or subjugated knowledges.

In the previous discussion about the text analogy and therapy, it was proposed that alternative stories can be generated or regenerated through a performance of meaning around unique outcomes. This performance of meaning around unique outcomes can also provide a basis for the identification of the subjugated knowledges and for the opening of space for the circulation of these knowledges. Again, the identification of these unique outcomes can be facilitated by the externalization of the problem.

Following the externalization of the unitary knowledges, unique outcomes can be located by an investigation of those aspects of the person's life, and those qualities that he or she experiences in relationships with others, that he/she can appreciate, but that do not fit with that which is specified by these unitary knowledges, that is, do not conform to the norms and expectations proposed by these knowledges. Persons can then be encouraged to discover what important messages these unique outcomes have for them about themselves and their relationships and to identify those "unique knowledges" that could accommodate these new realizations. Thus local, popular, or indigenous knowledges become available to be performed.

Erudite knowledges can also be identified through "archeological" endeavors. Persons can be invited to investigate their family and community archives, as well as those historical documents that might relate to the specific domains of their practices of life, in an attempt to locate previously established knowledges that fit with the unique outcomes and unique knowledges. In establishing these historical accounts of subjugated knowledges, and in inviting speculation about how space might be opened for the future performance and circulation of these knowledges, persons are able to appreciate their unique history of struggle and more explicitly embrace these knowledges in the constitution of their own lives and relationships. Thus, in therapy, as persons embrace these unique knowledges, we can witness, as Foucault puts it, the "insurrection of the subjugated knowledges."

ORAL AND WRITTEN TRADITIONS:
A DISTINCTION

This chapter has focused on some recent developments in so-cial theory, with particular reference to the text analogy, on Foucault's history of systems of thought, and in general terms, on the relevance of these developments to that activity commonly referred to as therapy. Although in our western culture the means of the institutionalized therapies are primarily and predominantly oral, we mostly emphasize the written tradition in this book. Let me briefly distinguish this from the oral tradition.

Clearly, speech and writing are different. Although it can be established that the spoken word preceded the written word in a historical sense, and that writing was founded on speech, it can also be established that, in literate societies, both traditions have evolved as independent forms. In referring to specific distinctions around written and spoken language, Stubbs (1980) concludes: "written language does not directly represent spoken language. It is evident from several facts that the two systems are at least partly autonomous" (p. 41). After reviewing some of the different forms of written language and its different relations with spoken language, Stubbs argues that:

> . . . we have to allow that in highly literate communities, at least for some people, the link between spoken and writ-ten language is markedly weakened, and written forms may lose something of their secondary character and gain more of an independent, primary character. (p. 41)

The "truth" status assigned to and the relative success of spoken and written languages is, to an extent, dependent upon the field of activity in question. Certainly, in many of the official domains of our society, getting it down in "black and white" is considered more prestigious. However, in other settings, "I will only believe this when I hear it from the horse's mouth" prevails. Despite this, there is a general mechanism at play in our culture that reinforces the importance of a writing dimension to our work. In many circumstances, writing achieves unsurpassed authority from the fact that it is not heard, but seen. In the western world there exists a time-honored tradition that privileges sight above the other senses — a tradition of "ocularcentrism."*

It is a cultural practice to place extraordinary trust on, and faith in, evidence that can be "seen" with the eye. This is reflected in our stock of adjectives for the attribution of "knowledge-able-ness" to persons and of adequacy to ideas. Those adjectives that we have available for such attribution are predominately, although not exclusively, ocular. For example, those persons who are presumed to have legitimate knowledge are considered to be "insightful," "perceptive," and "far-sighted." In contrast, those who are considered to lack these qualities are viewed as "blind" or "short-sighted." And those ideas that are most likely to be embraced are those judged to be "illuminating," "enlightening," and "visionary."

The Written Tradition

Stubbs (1980), in reviewing the contribution of a writing system, states that a society with such a system has "new intellectual resources which greatly facilitate thought," in that:

1. "Each generation no longer has to begin from scratch or from what the previous generation can remember and pass on."
2. Writing allows for the "accumulation of recorded wisdom."
3. Writing enables findings to be recorded in a form that "makes them easier to study and consider critically, and this in turn leads to more discoveries."
4. "The information content of written language is higher and less predictable."

---

*Many authors, particularly those of the French intellectual world, have identified the proliferation of "reason" with the tradition of ocularcentrism and have strongly critiqued this. Some, like Irigaray (1974), have proposed the privileging of other senses. Others, like Foucault, have been content to critique ocularcentric practices, such as the "normalizing gaze" and its subjugating effects.

5. Writing dramatically transforms the teacher-student relationship and promotes independence in thought, as "there can be knowledge without a knower, existing independently in books" (p. 107).

It can be argued that these proposed advantages are both overdrawn and culture specific. For example, it has been demonstrated that independent knowledge can exist in a community and be passed on by other means, including through the tradition of storytelling and through the medium of song and dance. For example, many of the knowledges of the Australian aboriginals existed in songlines, and with these they "sang their world into existence" over generations (Chatwin, 1988).

However, while accepting that Stubbs' findings do, to an extent, reflect ethnocentrism, we find support for the proposition that, in our culture, recourse to the written tradition in therapy promotes the formalization, legitimation, and continuity of local popular knowledges, the independent authority of persons, and the creation of a context for the emergence of new discoveries and possibilities.

The Written Tradition and Time

In order to perceive change in one's life—to experience one's life as progressing—and in order to perceive oneself changing one's life, a person requires mechanisms that assist her to plot the events of her life within the context of coherent sequences across time—through the past, present and future. Put another way, the detection of change is vital to the performance of meaning and to the experience of personal agency in one's life, and this detection of change is engendered by the introduction of a linear conception of time. Despite this, the temporal dimension has been much neglected in the therapy world.

As the "concept of time as linear requires the ability to record sequences of events" (Stubbs, 1980), and as writing is ideally suited to provide for such a recording, then it would appear that the written tradition is one important mechanism for the introduction of the linear conception of time, and thus for the generation of meaning in our lives. Persons who seek therapy frequently experience an incapacity to intervene in a life that seems unchanging; they are stymied in their search for new possibilities and alternative meanings. Consequently, it would seem that the written tradition, insofar as it facilitates the mapping of experience onto the temporal dimension, has much to offer to those activities defined as therapy.

Organization of Information

In drawing distinctions around spoken and written language in terms of the limitations imposed by focal consciousness, Chafe (1985) introduces the notion of "idea units." Idea units represent the extent of a person's short-term memory capacity, a capacity that fixes and limits the amount of information that one can attend to at any particular point in time:

> . . . an idea unit expresses what is held in short-term memory at a particular time, that short-term memory contains approximately the amount of information that can comfortably be expressed with about seven words of English, and that the content of short-term memory changes about every two seconds . . . " (p. 106)

According to Chafe, not only does written language free persons of the constraints established by the "limited temporal and informational capacity of focal consciousness," in that we have "time to let our attention roam over a large amount of information and devote itself to a more deliberate organisation of linguistic resources," but also provides the mechanism by which the informational content of idea units can be significantly increased, and by which these idea units can be reorganized in different "relations of dependence."

Thus, following Chafe's line, we could argue for the introduction of the written tradition in therapy, in that it potentially provides for an expansion of the information that can be processed in our short-term memory at any one point in time. It allows for the more "deliberate organization of linguistic resources" and the reorganization of "idea units" into different "relations of dependence." That is, it can be argued that writing provides one mechanism through which persons can be more active in determining the arrangement of information and experience and in producing different accounts of events and experience.

These comments regarding the utility of writing are as relevant to the reader as they are to the writer and as relevant to the therapist as they are to the person seeking therapy.

CONCLUSION

I have presented an overview of some recent developments in social theory, with attention to the text analogy and to Foucault's thought, detailed various proposals regarding the form of a therapy that is situated in these ideas, and argued for the incorporation of written means in therapy. This last proposal is by no means a new one. There is already some literature available that addresses this subject. I will not here attempt to summarize it here; those readers who wish to explore this literature might begin with Burton's "The Use of Written Productions in Psychotherapy" (1965).

With regard to the oral and written traditions, although David and I do not consciously rank one above the other in status, we do privilege the oral tradition in our work. We talk with most of the persons who seek our help, but we do not write to all or engage ourselves with all in the co-construction of written accounts of new stories.* Time pressures often limit our recourse to the written tradition. However, in reviewing the merit of this tradition, while writing this book, we have been forced to question the wisdom of being organized in such a way that time is often such a determining factor.

---

*This is not always the case. We have often worked through literate means with persons who request our assistance but who refuse to talk with anyone, and with those who even refuse to meet with anyone.

2. *Externalizing of the Problem*

"Externalizing" is an approach to therapy that encourages persons to objectify and, at times, to personify the problems that they experience as oppressive. In this process, the problem becomes a separate entity and thus external to the person or relationship that was ascribed as the problem. Those problems that are considered to be inherent, as well as those relatively fixed qualities that are attributed to persons and to relationships, are rendered less fixed and less restricting.

I (M. W.) began my first systematic attempts at encouraging persons to externalize their problems approximately ten years ago. These attempts took place predominantly within the context of work with families that presented for therapy with problems identified in children. Aspects of this work have been presented earlier (e.g., White, 1984, 1985, 1986 a, c).

The externalization of the child's problem clearly had great appeal for these families. Although the problem was usually defined as internal to the child, all family members were affected and often felt overwhelmed, dispirited and defeated. In various ways, they took the ongoing existence of the problem and their failed attempts to solve it as a reflection on themselves, each other, and/ or their relationships. The continuing survival of the problem and the failure of corrective measures served to confirm, for family members, the presence of various negative personal and relation-

This chapter originally appeared in the *Dulwich Center Newsletter*, Summer 1988/89.

ship qualities or attributes. Thus, when the members of these families detailed the problems for which they were seeking therapy, it was not at all unusual for them to present what I call a "problem-saturated description" of family life. Elsewhere, when drawing on the story or text analogy, I have posed this "problem-saturated description" as a "dominant story of family life" (White, 1988; also see Chapter 1).

In helping these family members separate themselves and their relationships from the problem, externalization opened up possibilities for them to describe themselves, each other, and their relationships from a new, nonproblem-saturated perspective; it enabled the development of an alternative story of family life, one that was more attractive to family members. From this new perspective, persons were able to locate "facts" about their lives and relationships that could not be even dimly perceived in the problem-saturated account of family life: "facts" that contradicted this problem-saturated account; facts that provided the nuclei for the generation of new stories. And, in the process, the child's problem was invariably resolved.

The very positive responses to these early systematic attempts at encouraging families to externalize their problems led me to extend this practice to a wide range of presenting problems. Throughout my subsequent explorations of this approach, I have found the externalization of the problem to be helpful to persons in their struggle with problems. Consequently, I have concluded that, among other things, this practice:

1. Decreases unproductive conflict between persons, including those disputes over who is responsible for the problem;
2. Undermines the sense of failure that has developed for many persons in response to the continuing existence of the problem despite their attempts to resolve it;
3. Paves the way for persons to cooperate with each other, to unite in a struggle against the problem, and to escape its influence in their lives and relationships;
4. Opens up new possibilities for persons to take action to retrieve their lives and relationships from the problem and its influence;

5. Frees persons to take a lighter, more effective, and less stressed approach to "deadly serious" problems; and
6. Presents options for dialogue, rather than monologue, about the problem.

Within the context of the practices associated with the externalizing of problems, neither the person nor the relationship between persons is the problem. Rather, the problem becomes the problem, and then the person's relationship with the problem becomes the problem.

As we have seen in Chapter 1, not only do the stories that persons have about their lives determine the meaning that they ascribe to experience, but these stories also determine which aspects of lived experience are selected out for the ascription of meaning. As Bruner (1986a) argues, it is not possible for narratives to encompass the full richness of our lived experience:

> . . . life experience is richer than discourse. Narrative structures organize and give meaning to experience, but there are always feelings and lived experience not fully encompassed by the dominant story. (p. 143)

Since the stories that persons have about their lives determine both the ascription of meaning to experience and the selection of those aspects of experience that are to be given expression, these stories are constitutive or shaping of persons' lives. The lives and relationships of persons evolve as they live through or perform these stories.

Through the lens of the text analogy, various assumptions can be made about persons' experience of problems. Here I make the general assumption that, when persons experience problems for which they seek therapy, (a) the narratives in which they are storying their experience and/or in which they are having their experience storied by others do not sufficiently represent their lived experience, and (b), in these circumstances, there will be significant and vital aspects of their lived experience that contradict these dominant narratives.

The externalizing of the problem enables persons to separate from the dominant stories that have been shaping of their lives and relationships. In so doing, persons are able to identify previously neglected but vital aspects of lived experience — aspects that could not have been predicted from a reading of the dominant story. Thus, following Goffman (1961), I have referred to these aspects of experience as "unique outcomes" (White, 1987, 1988).

As unique outcomes are identified, persons can be encouraged to engage in performances of new meaning in relation to these. Success with this requires that the unique outcome be plotted into an alternative story about the person's life. I have referred to this alternative story as a "unique account" and have developed an approach to questioning that encourages persons to locate, generate, or resurrect alternative stories that will "make sense" of the unique outcomes. Other questions inspire persons to investigate what these new developments might reflect about personal and relationship attributes and qualities. In the process of entertaining and responding to these questions, persons derive new and "unique redescriptions" of themselves and of their relationships (White, 1988). Unique redescription questions can also assist persons in the revision of their relationships with themselves (e.g., "In what way do you think these discoveries might affect your attitude towards yourself?"), in the revision of their relationship with others (e.g., "How might this discovery affect your relationship with . . . ?"), and in the revision of their relationship with problems (e.g., "In refusing to cooperate with the problem in this way, are you supporting it or undermining it?").

Questions that invite persons to extend the performance of these alternative stories can then be introduced. These prompt an investigation of some of the new and "unique possibilities" that can be expected to accompany the unique accounts and the unique redescriptions of persons and their relationships (White, 1988). The scope of these alternative stories can be further extended through the introduction of questions that invite persons to identify and recruit an audience to the performance of new meanings in their life. I have referred to these questions as "unique circulation" questions (see Chapter 1).

I believe that therapy informed by practices associated with the externalizing of problems facilitates the "re-authoring" (Myerhoff,

1986) of lives and relationships. Below, some of the practices associated with the externalizing of problems are described. Although details of these practices appear under different headings, readers will note that there is considerable overlap in the discussion under each of these.

RELATIVE INFLUENCE QUESTIONING

A general interviewing process that I have referred to as "relative influence questioning" (White, 1986a) is particularly effective in assisting persons to externalize the problem. This process of questioning is initiated at the outset of the first interview, so that persons are immediately engaged in the activity of separating their lives and relationships from the problem.

Relative influence questioning is comprised of two sets of questions. The first set encourages persons to map the influence of the problem in their lives and relationships. The second set encourages persons to map their own influence in the "life" of the problem. By inviting persons to review the effects of the problem in their lives and relationships, relative influence questions assist them to become aware of and to describe their relationship with the problem. This takes them out of a fixed and static world, a world of problems that are intrinsic to persons and relationships, and into a world of experience, a world of flux. In this world, persons find new possibilities for affirmative action, new opportunities to act flexibly.

Mapping the Influence of the Problem

Questions are introduced that encourage persons to map the influence of the problem in their lives and relationships. These questions assist persons to identify the problem's sphere of influence in the behavioral, emotional, physical, interactional, and attitudinal domains.

This involves a problem-saturated description of family life, which is much broader than the description that is usually offered of the problem "itself." Rather than restrict the investigation to the relationship between the problem and the person ascribed the problem, these questions identify the effect of the problem across various interfaces — between the problem and various persons, and between the problem and various relationships. This opens up a very broad field for the later search for unique outcomes and for the possibilities of affirmative action. Affirmative action might be taken across any of these interfaces. This makes it possible for all of those associated with the problem to experience a new sense of personal agency.

To illustrate the practice of "mapping the influence of the problem," I have selected the problem of encopresis. I believe that this is appropriate, as many of these practices originated in my work with families where children had histories of persistent and unremitting soiling.

Nick, aged six years, was brought to see me by his parents, Sue and Ron.* Nick had a very long history of encopresis, which had resisted all attempts to resolve it, including those instituted by various therapists. Rarely did a day go by without an "accident" or "incident," which usually meant the "full works" in his underwear.

To make matters worse, Nick had befriended the "poo." The poo had become his playmate. He would "streak" it down walls, smear it in drawers, roll it into balls and flick it behind cupboards and wardrobes, and had even taken to plastering it under the kitchen table. In addition, it was not uncommon for Ron and Sue to find soiled clothes that had been hidden in different locations around the house, and to discover poo pushed into various corners and squeezed into the shower and sink drains. The poo had even developed the habit of accompanying Nick in the bath.

In response to my questions about the influence of the poo in the lives and relationships of family members, we discovered that:

*To preserve confidentiality, all names are fictitious.

1. *The poo was making a mess of Nick's life by isolating him from other children and by interfering with his school work. By coating his life, the poo was taking the shine off his future and was making it impossible for him and others to see what he was really like as a person. For example, this coating of poo dulled the picture of him as a person, making it difficult for other people to see what an interesting and intelligent person he was.*

2. *The poo was driving Sue into misery, forcing her to question her capacity to be a good parent and her general capability as a person. It was overwhelming her to the extent that she felt quite desperate and on the verge of "giving up." She believed her future as a parent to be clouded with despair.*

3. *The ongoing intransigence of the poo was deeply embarrassing to Ron. This embarrassment had the effect of isolating him from friends and relatives. It wasn't the sort of problem that he could feel comfortable talking about to workmates. Also, the family lived in a relatively distant and small farming community, and visits of friends and relatives usually required that they stay overnight. These overnight stays had become a tradition. As Nick's "accidents" and "incidents" were so likely to feature in any such stay, Ron felt constrained in the pursuit of this tradition. Ron had always regarded himself as an open person, and it was difficult for him to share his thoughts and feelings with others and at the same time keep the "terrible" secret.*

4. *The poo was affecting all the relationships in the family in various ways. For example, it was wedged between Nick and his parents. The relationship between him and Sue had become somewhat stressed, and much of the fun had been driven out of it. And the relationship between Nick and Ron had suffered considerably under the reign of tyranny perpetrated by the poo. Also, since their frustrations with Nick's problems always took center stage in their discussions, the poo had been highly influential in the relationship between Sue and Ron, making it difficult for them to focus their attention on each other.*

Mapping the Influence of Persons

Once a description of the problem's sphere of influence has been derived by mapping its effects in persons' lives and relationships, a second set of questions can be introduced. This set features those questions that invite persons to map their influence and the influence of their relationships in the "life" of the problem. These questions bring forth information that contradicts the problem-saturated description of family life and assist persons in identifying their competence and resourcefulness in the face of adversity.

Ordinarily, it is very difficult for persons to locate examples of their own influence in the life of the problem. This is particularly so when they have suffered under longstanding and apparently intractable problems that they have experienced as eclipsing their lives and relationships. However, by this stage the identification of the influence of the problem has set the scene for the identification of the influence of persons. Persons are less transfixed by the problem and less constrained in their perception of events surrounding the problem. This facilitates the discovery of unique outcomes.

And, as previously mentioned, the mapping of the effects of the problem across various interfaces — between the problem and various persons, and between the problem and various relationships — opens up a very broad field in which to search for and identify unique outcomes. Thus, in the mapping of their influence in the life of the problem, persons are not restricted to the narrow focus of the relationship between the problem and the person or the relationship in which the problem was considered to reside.

For new information about previously neglected "facts" effectively to contradict the problem-saturated description of life, it must be considered significant to the persons concerned. Only if it is significant will it constitute a unique outcome for such persons. The prior mapping of the extent of the problem's influence facilitates the attribution of such significance. Any new piece of information about the influence of persons is thrown into sharp relief against this map. For example, it was only after mapping the influence of anorexia nervosa in her life and upon her relationships that a young woman was able to appreciate the profound significance of the fact that she had not allowed the problem to isolate her from friends.

When mapping the influence of family members in the life of what we came to call "Sneaky Poo," we discovered that:

1. *Although Sneaky Poo always tried to trick Nick into being his playmate, Nick could recall a number of occasions during which he had not allowed Sneaky Poo to "outsmart" him. These were occasions during which Nick could have cooperated by "smearing," "streaking," or "plastering," but declined to do so. He had not allowed himself to be tricked into this.*
2. *There was a recent occasion during which Sneaky Poo could have driven Sue into a heightened sense of misery, but she resisted and turned on the stereo instead. Also, on this occasion she refused to question her competence as a parent and as a person.*
3. *Ron could not recall an occasion during which he had not allowed the embarrassment caused by Sneaky Poo to isolate him from others. However, after Sneaky Poo's requirements of him were identified, he did seem interested in the idea of defying these requirements. In response to my curiosity about how he might protest against Sneaky Poo's requirements of him, he said that he might try disclosing the "terrible" secret to a workmate. (This intention is a unique outcome in that it could not have been predicted by a reading of the problem-saturated story of a family life.)*
4. *Some difficulty was experienced in the identification of the influence of family relationships in the life of Sneaky Poo. However, after some discussion, it was established that there was an aspect to Sue's relationship with Nick that she thought she could still enjoy, that Ron was still making some attempts to persevere in his relationship with Nick, and that Nick had an idea that Sneaky Poo had*

not destroyed all of the love in his relationship with his parents.

After identifying Nick's, Sue's, and Ron's influence in the life of Sneaky Poo, I introduced questions that encouraged them to perform meaning in relation to these examples, so that they might "reauthor" their lives and relationships.

How had they managed to be effective against the problem in this way? How did this reflect on them as people and on their relationships? What personal and relationship attributes were they relying on in these achievements? Did this success give them any ideas about further steps that they might take to reclaim their lives from the problem? What difference would knowing what they now knew about themselves make to their future relationship with the problem?

In response to these questions, Nick thought that he was ready to stop Sneaky Poo from outsmarting him so much, and decided that he would not be tricked into being its playmate anymore. Sue had some new ideas for refusing to let Sneaky Poo push her into misery, and Ron thought that he just might be ready to take a risk and follow up with his idea of telling a workmate of his struggle with Sneaky Poo.

I met with this family again two weeks later. In that time Nick had had only one minor accident—this described as light "smudging." Sneaky Poo had tried to win him back after nine days, but Nick had not given in. He had taught Sneaky Poo a lesson—he would not let it mess up his life anymore. He described how he had refused to be tricked into playing with Sneaky Poo and believed that his life was no longer coated with it, that he was now shining through. He was talkative, happier, felt stronger, and was more physically active. Sneaky Poo had been a tricky character, and Nick had done very well to get his life back for himself.

Sue and Ron had also "gotten serious" in their decision not to cooperate with the requirements of Sneaky Poo. Sue had started to "treat herself" more often, particularly on those occasions during which Sneaky Poo was giving her a hard time, and "had put her foot down," showing that it couldn't take her so lightly anymore.

Ron had taken a risk and had protested Sneaky Poo's isolation of him. He had talked to a couple of his workmates about the problem. They had listened respectfully, offering a few comments. An hour later, one of them had returned and had disclosed that he had been experiencing a similar problem with a son. There ensued a very significant conversation and a strengthening bond of friendship. And without that coating on Nick's life, Ron had discovered that "Nick was good to talk to."

I encouraged Nick, Sue, and Ron to reflect on and speculate about what this success said about the qualities that they possessed as people and about the attributes of their relationships. I also encouraged them to review what these facts suggested about their current relationship with Sneaky Poo. In this discussion, family members identified further measures that they could take to decline Sneaky Poo's invitations to support it.

We met on a third occasion three weeks later, and I discovered that all had proceeded to take further steps to outrun Sneaky Poo, steps to ensure that it would be put in its proper place. Nick had made some new friends and had been catching up on his school work, and the family had visited overnight with several friends and relatives. Sue was making good her escape from guilt. This had been facilitated, to an extent, by the fact that she and Ron had been talking more to other parents about the trials and tribulations of parenting. In so doing they had learned that they were not the only parents who had doubts about their parenting skills.

We then did some contingency planning, just in case Sneaky Poo tried to make a comeback and to outstreak Nick again. I saw this family again one month later for a review. At the six-month follow-up, Nick was doing very well. Only on one or two occasions had there been a slight smudging on his pants. He was more confident and doing even better with friends and at school. Everyone felt happy with his progress.

DEFINING THE PROBLEM
TO BE EXTERNALIZED

In the practices associated with externalizing the problem, care is taken to ensure that the persons' description of it and of its effects in their lives and relationships are privileged. After the problem has been described, the externalizing of it proceeds "naturally" from the mapping of its effects in persons' lives and in their relationships. This externalizing of the problem is further reinforced by the mapping of the influence of persons in the life of the problem.

Often, persons offer common and general definitions of the problems that are of concern to them. However, the details of the effects of these problems or the persons' experience of them are always unique. Thus, except in very general terms, it is not possible to predict the effects of the problem in advance of meeting with the persons concerned.

The definitions of problems that persons offer can be quite specific and behavioral (e.g., "He has a tantrum when") or they can be quite general (e.g., "We have a communication problem"). At other times, persons can have difficulty defining the problem in a way that fits their experience of it. On these occasions, the therapist may suggest several candidate definitions and then check with the person as to whether any of these definitions reasonably encapsulates his or her experience.

As with any approach to working with persons who seek therapy, it is important that therapists do not make generalizations about situations, but keep in mind the specifics of every circumstance and think ahead to the likely consequences of particular courses of action. This argues for a certain level of "consciousness" on the therapist's behalf. Further, lest the therapist inadvertently contribute to persons' experiences of oppression, this consciousness requires an appreciation of local politics—that is, politics at the level of relationships. This consciousness discourages therapists from inviting the externalizing of problems such as violence and sexual abuse. When these problems are identified, the therapist would be inclined to encourage the externalizing of the attitudes and beliefs that appear to compel the violence, and those strategies that maintain persons in their subjugation, for example, the enforcement of secrecy and isolation.

Definition as Fluid and Evolving

Although the external definition of the problem can remain fixed across the course of therapy, more often it is fluid and evolves through time. This is particularly the case when persons have been struggling to identify terms of description that adequately represent their experience of the problem. The evolution of problem definitions can be considerably facilitated by relative influence questioning. The following provides one example of how this process of questioning contributes to the evolution of the external definition of the problem.

Marjorie, a sole parent with two children, aged 10 and 11 years, sought therapy for what she described as tantrums in the family. When asked to clarify this, she stated that she thought that everyone, including herself, took frustrations out in the form of tantrums.

When asked about what she perceived to be the effects of these tantrums on her life, Marjorie said that they encouraged her to avoid conflict with the children. When asked about the effect of avoiding conflict in her relationships with her children, she suddenly identified the fact that this was forcing her to abdicate her rights. Did this mean that she often felt taken for granted? "Yes!" Marjorie exclaimed.

When asked what Marjorie thought could be making her vulnerable to the invitations of others to be a taken-for-granted person, "guilt" emerged as a likely culprit. The effect of guilt in her life was then more fully explored. Thus, guilt was a new external definition of the problem that struck a chord for her, one that encompassed vital aspects of her lived experience.

Aspects of Marjorie's influence in the life of guilt were then identified. Marjorie was encouraged to perform meaning in relation to these unique outcomes. She took steps to extend her own influence by protesting the effects of guilt and announcing her resignation from it. For the children, it was discovered that this guilt had been successful, to an extent, in its invitations for them to take Marjorie for granted. However, several occasions upon which the children had successfully declined these invitations were identified. This mother and her children quickly repossessed their lives and relationships.

From the Specific to the General

At times, as in the following example, when persons offer a highly specific definition of the problem, it can be helpful to encourage them to construct a more general external definition of it. This has the effect of broadening the field for the identification of the influence of the problem and for the location of unique outcomes.

The Smith family consulted me about their seven-year-old daughter, Mary, who had a longstanding "sleep problem." The parents, James and Rachel, were finding this problem very fatiguing. They had made exhaustive attempts to solve it without experiencing a "scrap" of success. These attempts had included consulting books, soliciting professional advice, and attending courses on parent effectiveness.

Rachel and James had found that the only viable way of dealing with this situation was for one of them to sit beside Mary, reassuringly holding her hand until she went to sleep. This often took over an hour and a half, and at times up to two and a half hours. Rachel and James were at their "wits' end."

As Rachel, James, and Mary could not recall an occasion when Mary went off to sleep by herself, it seemed unlikely that significant examples of their influence would be available in the restricted field that was provided by such a narrow and specific definition of the problem. Therefore, I introduced questions that encouraged the specification of a more general external problem and the identification of the broader field of the problem's influence.

As the sleep problem had Mary depending on her parents for reassurance, what effect did James and Rachel think this could be having on her life more generally? After some discussion, "insecurity" emerged as a more general external definition of the problem. Apart from the sleep problem, what other effects was insecurity having in Mary's life? Rachel said that insecurity was clearly making it difficult for Mary to deal directly with any conflicts she had with her peers. Under circumstances of such conflict, she would usually run to the nearest adult, visibly distressed and in need of assurance. This tended to happen more frequently when James and Rachel were present. In mapping the effects of this "insecurity" in James' and Rachel's lives and in their relationships with Mary, it was ascertained that it compelled them to intervene in such disputes on Mary's behalf.

When reviewing the influence of family members in relation to insecurity, I asked if anyone could recall an occasion when Mary could have allowed insecurity to push her into depending on her parents for reassurance, but she reassured herself instead. Immediately Rachel thought of a recent example in which she had noticed Mary doing some of her own problem-solving with a peer instead of running to her mother to do this for her.*

This opened the door for the introduction of questions that encourage the performance of new meanings. Had Mary noticed this, too? No, she hadn't. How did she think she might have done this? What had she done to get herself ready to make such a breakthrough? What was it like for her to discover that she had become a problem-solver? What else did it say about her ability? I canvassed the parents' opinions on these questions as well, and the responses brought forth a new description of Mary's competence and of her ability to reassure herself.

Mary was definite in her preference for this "new picture" of herself over the "old picture." What did her attraction to this new picture say about Mary's readiness for other steps to take her life away from insecurity? And how would this new knowledge of Mary's capacity to escape insecurity and reassure herself help Rachel and James defy the effects of insecurity in their relationship with her? In response to these questions, various possibilities were discussed and, over the next six weeks, Mary developed her capacity to reassure herself to the extent that she started to insist on getting herself off to sleep.

---

*Although an example of Mary's influence in the life of insecurity was quickly identified, such an example was not essential to the progress of the therapy. Alternatively, an example of the parents' influence in the life of insecurity could have been identified. Recently, when working with another family where a child had a similar problem, evidence of the child's influence in the life of insecurity was not immediately available, but evidence of the parents' refusal to cooperate with the dictates of insecurity was. On this occasion, they had demanded that the child reassure herself. Family members were engaged in a performance of meaning in relation to this unique outcome, and before the end of the session the child seemed happy that, on this occasion, her parents had firmly taken her side against insecurity.

From "Expert" to "Popular" Definitions

At times, especially when persons have been encouraged to use "scientific classification" to describe their concerns, persons offer problem definitions in terms that are informed by "expert knowledge." These retranscriptions of problem definitions serve to decontextualize problems and thus detract fom the available options for persons to intervene in the "life" of problems. They do not provide definitions that enable persons to review their relationships with the problem or allow for unique outcomes to be identified. Thus, these retranscriptions frequently diminish the possibilities for persons to experience a sense of personal agency.

It is often important to encourage persons to construct alternative definitions of problems: definitions that are most relevant to their experience; definitions that enable them to address more adequately their immediate concerns. The following example provides an account of the derivation of an external definition of the problem that was relevant to the experience of family members concerned.

Jim was brought to see me by his worried parents. Some seven years previously he had been diagnosed "schizophrenic." Mr. and Mrs. Brown were becoming increasingly concerned about the extent of Jim's dependence on them. He was entirely reclusive and demonstrated little interest in modifying his career in life. In response to his parents' questions about why he wasn't doing something with his life, he would habitually respond, "It is the schizophrenia."

I asked Jim if he had any concerns about how things were going in his life, and he said that he did not think so. When asked what he understood about the condition of his life, he said that he had "schizophrenia, and that is all there is to it."

I then encouraged Mrs. and Mr. Brown to describe the effect of schizophrenia in the lives and relationships of family members. In relation to Jim's life, they believed that it was giving him bad habits. I asked them to describe these habits and then to provide me with some examples about the effects of these. I summarized with, "so, these habits that schizophrenia is coaching in Jim's life are turning him into a passenger with an indirect life."

I turned to Jim, and asked if he thought this was the case. He said that he didn't know. In response, I asked, "If it were the case that these habits were turning you into a passenger and standing in the way of your directing your own life, would this be of concern to you?" "Yes, it would," Jim answered. "Why would this be of concern to you?" I inquired. In responding to this and subsequent questions, Jim began to identify and articulate his own concerns and his experience of various problems. He also began to "perform" an argument to challenge the impoverishing effects that these problems were having in his life.

Facilitating a Mutually Acceptable Definition of the Problem

At times, when families or couples present for therapy, persons are in considerable dispute over the definition of the problem. These disputes make it difficult for them to work cooperatively in any attempt to challenge the effects of problems in their lives and relationships. In these circumstances, externalizing can establish a mutually acceptable definition of the problem and facilitates conditions under which persons can work effectively together to resolve their problems. Elsewhere, I have provided various examples of this practice (e.g., White, 1984, 1986c).

This facet of externalizing the problem is particularly important when working with conflicted couples and with the families of rebellious adolescents.

John and Wendy made an appointment with the intention of addressing concerns that they had about their son's "irresponsibility." Joe, 16 years of age, had, somewhat reluctantly, conformed to their wishes for him to accompany them. However, he did not agree that his parents had good reason to be concerned about him. In fact, Wendy and John's decision to make the appointment had confirmed for him what he believed to be the problem all along — his parents' excessive "nagging" and "hassling" of him.

Attempting to sidestep this unproductive dispute over how the problem was to be defined, I asked John and Wendy what they thought might happen if things did not change. In response, they talked at some length about how anxious they felt about the likely quality of Joe's future. I then asked how this anxiety was organizing them around Joe's life. It was encouraging them to watch over him more closely and, in various other ways, had them centering their lives around Joe's. "What effect was this anxiety having on Joe's life?"

Joe soon joined into the spirit of this inquiry. He identified that this anxiety about his future was crowding him and making it difficult for him to have his own life. Was this a problem to him? Yes, it was. Didn't being watched over appeal to him? No, it didn't. Would he be interested in joining his parents to undermine this anxiety and its effects in their relationships? Yes, he would.

Establishing a mutually acceptable definition of an external problem had set the scene for a cooperative endeavor. Wendy, John, and Joe worked together to identify more fully the effect of the anxiety in their lives and relationships; as they mapped their influence in the "face of this anxiety," various unique outcomes were located. One of these included a recent step that Joe had taken to undermine his parents' insecurity about his future. A performance of meaning around unique outcomes was initiated, and Joe, John, and Wendy began to explore new options for intervening in their lives and relationships.

UNIQUE OUTCOMES

In the Sneaky Poo example, unique outcomes were identified in most of the relationships between the problem and family members, and in the relationships between the problem and the relationships of family members. However, it is often difficult to identify unique outcomes across all possible interfaces and, although this is helpful, its achievement is not at all necessary. It is only necessary that one unique outcome be identified in order to facilitate performances of new meaning.

And, although it is helpful if all of those persons who have a relationship with the problem are actively engaged in performing new meanings in relation to one or more unique outcomes, this is not a necessary condition either. If one person is actively engaged in such a performance, and if this person is able to decline all invitations to cooperate with the problem that are inadvertently extended by others, then this will significantly undermine the problem.

Once details of the effects of the problem have been established, it becomes easier for persons to specify their own influence in relation to the problem. For instance, it was established that Sneaky Poo was driving Sue into misery. Details about what misery meant to Sue were then elicited. Later, when I introduced questions that encouraged family members to map their own influence, Sue was able to identify an occasion in which Sneaky Poo did not have quite these effects on her. The details of the effects of the problem help the therapist to be quite specific in the construction of these questions.

Historical Unique Outcomes

Unique outcomes can be identified through a historical review of the persons' influence in relation to the problem. Here persons can be encouraged to recall "facts" or events that contradict the problem's effects in their lives and in their relationships. Although such events are experienced by the persons concerned at the time of their occurrence, the problem-saturated stories of their lives usually rule out the attribution of new meanings to such experiences. These historical unique outcomes can facilitate performances of new meanings in the present, new meanings that enable persons to reach back and to revise their personal and relationship histories.

Katherine, 26 years of age, had seriously injured her back when she was 13 years old. Apart from the physical restriction, this injury had resulted in considerable and persistent pain. This pain had not responded to the many subsequent investigations and various treatments. From the time of the accident, Katherine had experienced a deterioration in her life, and when referred to me, she was suffering considerably from anxiety and depression.

Katherine was accompanied to the first meeting by her mother, Joan. I encouraged them to map the influence of the pain in their lives and their relationships. One of the many complications the pain had contributed to Katherine's life was that it had isolated her from contact with strangers. While encouraging Katherine and Joan to map their influence, I asked Katherine if she could recall a time when she could have let pain prevent her from having personal contact with another person but refused to submit to its demands. After a search that lasted about 20 minutes, Katherine remembered an incident that had occurred three years earlier. She had been for a short walk and, not far from home, had noticed a stranger approaching from the opposite direction. The stranger looked friendly, and Katherine thought that he might greet her. As he drew level, she nodded and said "hello" as he passed. Although this was a feat that she could not have predicted in advance, she did not attach any significance to it at the time.

I encouraged both Katherine and Joan to perform meaning around this event. How did Katherine cope with her anxiety as the stranger approached? How did she stop it from turning her back? What had she done to prepare herself for this? If she had understood the significance of this at the time, what would this have reflected about her progress? What would this have told her about herself that she could have appreciated? What difference would it have made if she had been more fully in touch with the significance of this achievement?

The identification of this historically located unique outcome constituted a turning point for both Katherine and Joan in the present, three years after the event. Various other unique outcomes then became available for inspection, including those that related to Joan's occasional refusal to participate in "pain journalism." Over a number of months, Katherine experimented with extending her influence and testing her newfound knowledge and developed a network of friends and a thirst for life. And Joan began to look more to her "own needs."

A subcategory of these historical unique outcomes is comprised of those that occur between sessions, or those that can be framed within the context of the history of the therapy. These provide a very fertile source for the performance of new meanings and for the generation of new stories.

Gail had been diagnosed with schizophrenia some years before my first contact with her. Despite numerous treatments, she had been restricted to an "in-the-corner lifestyle," with auditory hallucinations remaining a significant problem. She called these hallucinations her "voices" and complained that they constantly harassed her.

In our first meeting, Gail identified evidence of her competence in the face of this harassment, and she started to take steps to extend her influence, challenging the voices in various ways and, for the most part, reducing them to the level of quiet thoughts.

Gail had informed me that the voices were opposed to my meetings with her. They would give her a particularly hard time before our appointments, doing their best to turn her back. On a couple of occasions, they had nearly succeeded. In attempting to help me understand this, Gail proposed that the voices were threatened by our meetings and desperate to avoid them at any cost.

Prior to one meeting, when Gail had very substantially reclaimed herself from the voices, they attempted a comeback and intensified their harassment of her. In response to this, Gail had become quite distressed, fearing that the voices were claiming her again. Perceiving that the new story of Gail's life was entering the shadow of the old story, I immediately introduced questions that I hoped would enable her to retrieve the new story. Some of these questions were informed by my knowledge of the history of Gail's struggle with the voices through the course of therapy.

How had she managed to defy the voices' influence on this recent occasion and bring herself to the appointment? She had told them to "shut up." I asked, "Not long ago, when the voices gave you a hard time about these meetings, what effect did they have on you?" "They had me in tears," replied Gail. "Did they get you into tears today?" "No, they didn't." "So what's the difference between you as a person now and you as a person then?" "I'm more capable!" "Why don't you tell the voices more about that?" "All right . . ."

Gail recovered from the shakiness of the previous weeks, quickly reducing the voices to quiet thoughts. At the next session, two *weeks later, Gail told me that she had gone from "strength to strength" and had not allowed the voices to harass her again. This was yet another turning point in Gail's life.*

Current Unique Outcomes

Some unique outcomes present themselves in the course of the session. These are usually brought to the persons' attention by the therapist's curiosity about them and by her/his invitations to such persons to render them sensible. The immediacy of these current unique outcomes is highly compelling, and they are directly available to persons for the performance of the new meanings.

Bette had managed to persuade Keith to attend therapy under the guise that she had some problems that she wanted addressed, and that she wanted the therapist to have access to his thoughts and his opinions about these. However, it was quickly apparent that the overriding problem was Keith's occasional violence and persistent aggression. From an investigation of the effects of the violence and aggression on Bette and on the relationship, it became clear to both partners that addressing this issue would have to be given priority. After some discussion, Keith agreed to participate.

An escape plan was derived, one that would be activated whenever Bette felt threatened and believed she was at risk of further violence. The installation of this escape plan would actively involve Keith. He would be required, ahead of time, to meet with any friends and relatives who might be included in the plan; in breaking the silence in relation to the violence, he would be making a significant contribution to the resolution of this problem. (This would be a unique outcome.)

After considerable discussion, Keith agreed to the idea. Through a process of questioning, Keith's aggression was located within the context of dominant knowledges that specify men's relationships with women, and within the context of power techniques that accompany these knowledges. Unique outcomes were identified in relation to the domination of these knowledges and techniques of power, and I engaged Keith and Bette in a performance of new meaning.

At about the halfway mark of our second session, Bette took a risk and expressed an opinion that she knew would be contrary to Keith's. Seconds went by, and although Keith was clearly struggling with himself, he did not react. I asked, "How did you do it? I would never have predicted this at this stage." "How did I do what?" replied Keith. "How did you stop yourself from reacting and trying to control what Bette was saying?" "I don't know." "Aren't you surprised by this?" "Well, I suppose that I am . . . Yeah, I am!" "What do you think this means?" "Well, er . . . " We explored the significance of this unique outcome for the rest of the session. And in this process there evolved a new account of Keith as a person.

Future Unique Outcomes

Unique outcomes can have a future location. These can be identified in a review of persons' intentions or plans to escape the influence of the problem or through an investigation of their hopes of freeing their lives and relationships from certain problems.

Although Nathan found it difficult to identify his influence in the life of the problem, he was disconcerted by discovering the extent of the problem's influence in his life. So disconcerted was he, in fact, that he became visibly determined to do something about the corner into which he had been pushed by the problem.

In response, I asked some questions. "You look as if you feel determined to do something about it." He was resolute. "What could you do to salvage your life?" He already had a couple of ideas. "Where did you get these ideas from?" "If you saw yourself acting on these ideas, what difference would that make to how you feel about yourself?" A great deal. "If you got to feel like this, what would you find easier to do in your life?" Nathan thought of several possibilities.

As Nathan entertained these questions, he became aware of the availability of an alternative and more rewarding account of him-

self as a person. Nathan followed through by taking steps to put this alternative account into circulation.

Although these unique outcomes relate to an anticipation of events to come, they are also current and can lead to the identification of historical unique outcomes. The existence of these intentions and hopes can be considered a present act of defiance in the "face" of the problem and can also lead to an investigation of those historical experiences that have informed persons that things might be different in the future—perhaps what they might have "glimpsed" that has kept their hopes alive.

Unique Outcomes and Imagination

Imagination plays a very significant part in the practices of externalizing the problem, both for the therapist and for those persons who have sought therapy. This is particularly important in the facilitation of conditions for the identification of unique outcomes and for the performance of meaning in relation to them.

It is important that the therapist imagine what could possibly be significant to the person seeking help and not be blinded by his/her own criteria of what would signify new developments in her/his life and relationships. For example, greeting a visitor to one's home may not be at all significant to the therapist in her/his own life, but to some persons this is a feat of very considerable significance—perhaps equivalent to the therapist's taking a walk on a tightrope. All such feats can be considered to be spectacular in nature. It is never the size of the step that a person takes that counts, but its direction.

As the therapist gains knowledge of persons' habitual and predictable responses to events surrounding the problem, he or she can imagine what sort of response might constitute a unique and unexpected outcome. This enhances the therapist's receptivity to "news of difference" and, in turn, assists him/her to recruit the imagination of those persons who seek therapy.

Bruce, who was diagnosed with schizophrenia some eight years previously, was brought to see me by his parents, Richard and

Mim. Bruce's younger sister, Eileen, also attended the meeting. Mim and Richard were concerned about the direction of Bruce's life. Although he was stable, he had become entirely withdrawn. He rarely emerged from his bedroom and hid from all visitors.

At the end of the first session, Bruce thought that he was ready to extend his own influence. He planned to call the coordinator of a low-key socialization group and arrange a time to meet. Bruce had been given the telephone number of this coordinator several times, but had never felt able to follow through with the call. He had not answered a telephone in five years, let alone made a call. I engaged Bruce and his parents in some debate about whether he was ready to make the call and wondered aloud whether it might be wiser for him to take some other preliminary steps, to help him get ready for this step. However, Bruce was sure that he was ready to make the call.

When the family returned for the next appointment, I asked that members catch me up on any developments. Apparently there were none. Things were "just the same." It wasn't until about halfway through the session that I recalled Bruce's resolve to call the coordinator of the socialization group. Had he made the call? "Yes," he said, and then went on to talk about something unrelated. I glanced around the room. Everybody seemed preoccupied with other things—all in different worlds. It was understandable that they would not be expecting anything different to happen.

"Wait, wait!" I said, "Did I hear what I thought I heard?" "What?" said Bruce. "Maybe schizophrenia is contagious, and I'm hearing things." I had Bruce's attention. "What?" he puzzled. "Well, for a while there, I thought that you said that you had gone ahead with that call." "You are not hearing things, that's what I did say," said Bruce reassuringly. "Then tell me again, only this time tell me a little louder so that the news sinks in!" Bruce promptly did so. I apologized, saying that I hadn't really expected this development, and then asked Bruce whether he would mind terribly letting me have the news one more time. This he did, and with that I pretended to fall off my chair.

Bruce was amused. Now everyone was attending to developments in Bruce's life. "Who else here had been unprepared for this news?" "Was anyone else surprised?" Richard reflected on these *questions, turned to Mim, and said, "Come to think of it, it is rather surprising, isn't it?" Mim immediately joined with the spirit of discovery and started asking Bruce questions about the events surrounding this unexpected behavior. Over the next 30 minutes, fired by curiosity, we all asked Bruce questions and speculated about the significance of this achievement. I recorded the questions, the responses to these, and the speculation that was entered into, and sent the family a summary of this in letter form.*

At our next meeting, one month later, I was quickly informed at the outset of the session that Bruce had surprised Mim on two occasions. Since we only had one hour for the meeting, we didn't get to investigate fully the incidents that related to both of these events or their entire significance. Over subsequent meetings, we all fell further behind Bruce, despite our very best efforts to keep abreast of the new developments in his life.

THE REVISION OF PERSONS' RELATIONSHIPS WITH PROBLEMS

The problem and its effects are linked in a relation of dependence. Thus, taking one-half of this relation, it could be said that the problem is dependent upon its effects for its survival. Elsewhere, I have suggested that these effects constitute the problem's life-support system; that is, these effects can be considered to represent requirements of the problem for its survival (White, 1986a).

The identification of unique outcomes and the performance of new meaning around these help persons to identify their resistance to the effects of the problem or its requirements. Considering the relation of dependence between the problem and its effects, it follows that, if persons refuse to cooperate with the requirements of the problem, then they are undermining it; refusing to submit to the effects of the problem renders the problem less effective. Thus, in the process of performing new meaning around unique outcomes, persons revise their relationship with the problem. The description of this revised relationship contrasts markedly with the description of the relationship between the problem and persons initially derived from the mapping of the influence of the problem. The exploration of new possibilities is enhanced if persons are encouraged to become more aware of this shift in their relationship with the problem and to articulate it explicitly.

The Harrisons sought therapy in relation to their son Aaron, eight years of age. His habit of throwing tantrums was a pressing problem, as was his tendency to wander off in the middle of the night. Everyone was convinced that he was becoming more uncontrollable as he was getting older.

There were other problems that concerned the Harrisons. These included Aaron's eating habits, his lack of cooperation, and his disorderly behavior at school. Aaron's eating behavior was indeed spectacular. Given half a chance, he would eat a whole jar of coffee, consume a tube of toothpaste, or drink a whole bottle of soy sauce in one shot. He had sabotaged a recent psychological assessment by eating the testing equipment.

Aaron had a long history of learning problems and was in a special education class. In addition, he had been diagnosed with hyperactivity at a young age. In contrast to Aaron, his elder sisters seemed relatively normal young women. Even their eating habits were not out of the ordinary.

When we mapped the influence of the family members in the life of the problem, the most recent and dramatic unique outcome had to do with Mrs. Harrison's "tuning-out" during one of Aaron's tantrums, rather than joining with it. Encouraging a performance of meaning in relation to this unique outcome, I asked what this meant with regard to Mrs. Harrison's relationship with the tantrums. By refusing to subject herself to the effects of the problem in this way, was she complying with the problem's requirements of her or defying them? Which relationship to the problem was she most attracted to? Would this noncooperative relationship with the problem strengthen it or weaken it? What else might she do to side with this new relationship with the problem rather than the old relationship? Was she now the more effective partner in this new relationship?

Over a few sessions, Mrs. Harrison transformed her relationship with the problem. Other family members followed suit and soon the tantrums were without a life-support system. Aaron's behavior substantially improved, his learning accelerated dramatically, and his ability to concentrate increased significantly. To my delight, Mrs. Harrison became a "consultant" to the other parents who had children in Aaron's class at school, and she assisted them to review their relationships with the various problems that were of concern to them.

RESPONSIBILITY

While practices associated with the externalizing of problems enable persons to separate themselves and their relationships from such problems, these practices do not separate persons from responsibility for the extent to which they participate in the survival of the problem. In fact, as these practices help persons become aware of and describe their relationship with the problem, they enable them to assume responsibility for the problem, something they could not do beforehand.

The practices associated with the externalizing of problems also (a) free persons from problem-saturated descriptions of their lives and relationships, (b) encourage the generation or resurrection of alternative and more rewarding stories of lives and relationships, and (c) assist persons to identify and develop a new relationship with the problem. In so doing, these practices foster a new sense of personal agency; with this, persons are able to assume responsibility for the investigation of new choices in their lives and to pursue new possibilities. In the process, they experience a newfound capacity to intervene in their world.

THE CULTURAL CONTEXT

When persons learn to separate from problems, they may come to challenge other practices, cultural in origin, that are "objectifying" or "thingifying" of persons and their bodies. Within the context of these practices, persons are constructed as objects and are encouraged to relate to themselves, their bodies, and to other persons as objects. This is fixing and formalizing of persons. In western societies, these objectifying practices are pervasive.

The practices associated with the externalizing of problems can be considered counter-practices that engage persons in the "de-objectification" of themselves, their bodies, and each other. Invariably, these counter-practices have great appeal to persons. They enthusiastically embrace them and find them liberating. In follow-up sessions, when we have discussed with persons their experience of the externalizing of the problem, many have remarked that it made immediate sense to them and that it had the effect of "freeing" them to act independently of the problem.

Michel Foucault, a French intellectual who regarded himself as an "historian of systems of thought," has traced the history of these cultural practices of objectification of persons for the purposes of "subjugation" (Foucault, 1965, 1973, 1979). According to Foucault, in recent history, western society has increasingly relied on the practices of the objectification of persons and their bodies to improve and extend social control. The modern history of the objectification of persons and their bodies coincides with the proliferation of what can be referred to as the "dividing practices" (Foucault, 1965) and the practices of "scientific classification" (Foucault, 1973). Foucault has traced the history of those dividing practices, which first emerged on a grand scale in the 17th century, heralded by the opening of the Hôpital Général in Paris in 1656. These practices enabled the exclusion of persons and of groups of persons, and the objectification of these persons through the ascription of personal and social identity. And under the practices of scientific classification, the body came to be constructed as a thing.

These practices were specifying of the identity of persons. And the specification of personhood that they introduced was highly individual — a specification for "self-possession" and "self-containment." Foucault is not alone in his observations of the increasing emphasis on the individual specification of personhood in the recent history of western culture. For example, Geertz (1976) emphasizes a similar point:

> The Western conception of the person as a bounded, unique cognitive universe, a dynamic centre of awareness, emotion, judgement and action organized into a distinctive whole is, however incorrigible it may seem to us, a rather peculiar idea within the concept of the world's cultures. (p. 225)

Foucault argues that this development is inextricably intertwined with and essential to the operation of power in the modern state, in the government of persons and of the bodies of persons, in the "subjugation" of persons, and in the forging of persons as "docile bodies." Rabinow, in summarizing Foucault's position, writes:

> The power of the state to produce an increasingly totalizing web of control is intertwined with and dependent on its ability to sproduce an increasing specification of individuality. (1984, p. 22)

Thus, in reviewing the cultural practices that constitute persons and the bodies of persons as objects, we are brought to a consideration of the operation of power in a particularly modern form. A review of this form of power will help us to understand the wider context of persons' experiences of subjugation. Such a review can also contribute to the generation of "therapies" of counter-practices. By way of providing such a review, I will discuss Foucault's (1979) analysis of Jeremy Bentham's Panopticon.

THE PANOPTICON

Structure

The Panopticon was an architectural form developed by Jeremy Bentham in the 18th century. Bentham proposed this architectural form as an "ideal" model for the organization or arrangement of persons in space that would effectively "forge" them as "docile bodies" — bodies that could be more easily transformed and used. He considered it ideal in that it would maximize the efficiency of persons while simultaneously minimizing the efforts required to supervise them. Thus, the Panopticon was envisioned as a model for a very economic form of power.

The technology of power around which the Panopticon was proposed was not entirely new. Rather, it took up and refined those techniques of control that had been developed at the local level — in the military camps, monasteries, schools, etc. As an architectural form, the Panopticon featured a circular building with a courtyard at the center or a series of buildings arranged around a courtyard. The building could have several levels, with each level the thickness of one room only. Every level was divided into small spaces, and each of these had a rear window that let in natural light and a large opening towards the front that faced onto the courtyard. There were no windows inserted laterally, between the various rooms, and thus the occupants of these rooms could not have direct contact with each other. These spaces could be designated as "cells," "workrooms," etc., depending upon the nature and the purpose of the organization.

The Gaze

Each of these individual spaces faced an observation tower that was situated in the center of the courtyard. This tower housed the guardians, and its levels corresponded exactly with the levels of the circular building. From this tower the guardians of the organization could have an uninterrupted view of all the activities taking place in the individual spaces. The guardians' view was facilitated by the backlighting of each space, the activities of persons in the spaces being silhouetted and thrown into sharp relief. Nothing could escape scrutiny. The persons in the spaces were to be the objects of perpetual observation. These spaces were: " . . . small theatres, in which each actor is alone, perfectly individualized and constantly visible" (Foucault, 1979, p. 200).

However, while the persons in these spaces were ever visible to the guardians in the tower, the guardians were never visible to the persons in the individual spaces. The tower was designed so that, through a careful arrangement of windows and doors, those in the individual spaces could not see into the tower. Those persons in the spaces could never detect whether they were being observed at any particular point in time. Such persons had little choice but to assume that they were the subject of a guardian's gaze at any time. Thus, they experienced themselves as the subjects of the ever-present gaze. This mechanism of power had the effect of "inciting" persons to act as if they were always being observed.

This was to be a very effective system of surveillance, as well as a very economic one, in that relatively few guardians, moving from one observation window to another, were required for its functioning.

"It is the fact of constantly being seen, of being able always to be seen, that maintains the disciplined individual in his subjection" (Foucault, 1979, p. 187).

Evaluation and the Fixing of Lives

The arrangement of persons in space that was afforded by the Panopticon facilitated the conditions under which these persons could, according to the norms constructed by the organization, be classified, qualified, measured, compared, differentiated, and judged. This enabled persons to be thought of as individual cases. Further, this spatial arrangement of persons provided ideal conditions for the training and correcting of persons according to these norms.

Thus, the ever-present gaze experienced by the persons occupying the individual spaces was in effect a "normalizing gaze." Those persons would experience themselves as being constantly evaluated according to the rules and norms specified by the organization. This normalizing gaze would subject persons to a "whole micro-penalty of time, of activity, of behaviour, of speech, of the body, of sexuality" (1979, p. 178).

The documentation of lives that became available through the invention of the file enhanced the practices of the normalization and the individualization of persons. This enabled individuals to be "captured and fixed in writing" and facilitated the gathering of statistics and the fixing of norms — that is, the construction of unitary and global knowledges about persons. According to Foucault, the description of persons, the "turning of real lives into writing," became an important mechanism in this new form of social control:

> Where religions once demanded the sacrifice of bodies, knowledge now calls for experimentation on ourselves, calls us to the sacrifice of the subject of knowledge. (1984c, p. 96)

In facilitating registration and the "objectification and subjectification" of persons, the file was instrumental in the "formalization of the individual."

Normalizing Judgment

The Panopticon was a model for the complete and successful subjugation of persons. Not only did each person feel under scrutiny at all times in relation to the rules and norms of the organization, but each person was also isolated in his/her experience of scrutiny, in subjugation to "normalizing judgment." Since it was not possible for the persons in the individual spaces to have direct contact with each other, it was not possible for them to compare experiences, to generate alternative knowledges, and to establish coalitions that would enable them to protest this subjugation. In this strictly hierarchical system of observation, in this "individualizing pyramid," the struggle and resistance that usually accompany "multiplicity" could not be initiated. Counter-power was thus effectively neutralized.

The Panopticon provides a model for a particularly modern system of power that relies on the technique of "normalizing judgment." It does not provide for a system of social control in which persons are judged according to their worth on moral grounds, one in which consequences are determined according to the extent to which someone has "wronged." Instead, it provides for a system of social control in which persons' performances are judged according to certain standards or specifications. Meticulous examination replaces moral judgment. Consequences are determined according to the person's level of performance. Here, it is not an offense to "do wrong," but an offense "not to reach the required level, or to fail with a task." All departures from the norm and the rule are punishable.

Self-subjugation

This modern system of power is one that not only renders persons and their bodies as objects, but also recruits persons into an active role in their own subjugation, into actively participating in operations that shape their lives according to the norms or specifications of the organization.

As previously discussed, never knowing when they were being subject to scrutiny, persons could only feel secure in their existence if they were to assume that they were the subjects of perpetual surveillance. Under these conditions they would become ever-vigilant with regard to their own behavior, evaluating all actions and gestures against the norms specified by the particular organization. And upon identifying any anomalies or aberrations in their own conduct, they would be induced to relate to their own bodies as objects, that is, to engage in disciplinary and corrective operations to forge their own bodies as docile. Thus, they became their own guardians. They policed their own gestures. And they became the objects of their own scrutiny.

> He who is subjected to a field of visibility, and who knows it, assumes responsibility for the constraints of power; he makes them play spontaneously upon himself; he inscribes himself in the power relation in which he simultaneously plays both roles; he becomes the principle of his own subjugation. (1979, p. 202)

A Positive Form of Power

Foucault argues that the Panopticon provides a model of power that is positive in character and in its effects, rather than negative.

When discussing the positive character of power, Foucault is not making reference to "positive" in the usual sense, that is, as something desirable or beneficial. Rather, he is referring to a form of power that is positive in the sense that it is constitutive or shaping of persons' lives. This notion of a power that is positive in its effects contrasts directly with common conceptions of power. Such conceptions propose that power is repressive in its operations and in its effects, that it principally disqualifies, limits, denies, and contains, and that it is of negative force and character.

Foucault argues that, in western society, we do not predominately experience the effects of a negative or repressive power; rather, we experience the effects of a positive power, one that is constitutive of the lives of persons. Through this power, persons are subject to normalizing "truths" that shape their lives and relationships. These "truths" are, in turn, constructed or produced in the operation of power.

> We must cease once and for all to describe the effects of power in negative terms; it "excludes," it "represses," it "censors," it "abstracts," it "masks," it "conceals." In fact power produces; it produces reality; it produces domains of objects and rituals of truth. The individual and the knowledge that may be gained from him belong to this production. (1979, p. 194)

When discussing "truths," Foucault is not subscribing to the belief that there exist objective or intrinsic facts about the nature of persons, but referring to constructed ideas that are accorded a truth status. These "truths" are "normalizing" in the sense that they construct norms around which persons are incited to shape or constitute their lives. Therefore, these are "truths" that are actually specifying of persons' lives.

Sovereign Power Versus Modern Power

Foucault also contrasted the modern form of power that informed the development of the Panopticon with an earlier form of power—that is, "sovereign power." The effectiveness of this earlier power was largely dependent on the extent to which the sovereign could be made visible to the populace; persons primarily experienced the power of the state through the visibility of the sovereign. Various mechanisms were utilized for turning the "spotlight" on the sovereign, for impressing the power of the state upon the populace, not the least of which were ceremony and spectacle. Thus, power was most intense at its point of origination.

Under the sovereign, the subjects of power were invisible. Those who most keenly experienced this power were those who were locked away in dungeons, hidden from sight. The capacity to banish was a measure of the effectiveness of this form of power. Sovereign power proved to be a very expensive and relatively ineffective form of social control.

In contrast to this, the success of the mechanism of power represented in the Panopticon was largely dependent upon rendering the source of power invisible to its subjects. In this form of power, it is the subjects who find themselves in the spotlight. The effectiveness of this form of power is measured by the extent to which its subjects are made ever-visible. Thus, this form of power is most intense, not at its point of origination, but at its point of contact. This provided for a very economical and effective form of social control.

> In short, to substitute for a power that is manifested through the brilliance of those who exercise it, a power that insidiously objectifies those on whom it is applied; to form a body of knowledge about these individuals, rather than to deploy the ostentatious signs of sovereignty. (1979, p. 220)

The Panopticon is also a model for a mechanism of power that is self-maintaining and highly autonomous in its operation. The guardians of the Panopticon are themselves objects of this power. Of the many visitors to the tower, it is not possible for the guardians to determine which are in fact supervisors. Thus, they experience subjection to ongoing evaluation by persons who are not visible to them, and they too are incited to operate on themselves according to the norms specified for their conduct. Thus, the

Panopticon provides for a mechanism in which all persons are simultaneously a subject of and an instrument, or vehicle, of power.*

> This indeed is the diabolical aspect of the idea and all the applications of it. One doesn't have here a power which is wholly in the hands of one person who can exercise it alone and totally over the others. It's a machine in which everyone is caught, those who exercise power just as much as those over whom it is exercised. (1980, p. 156)

Discussion

The Panopticon, as an architectural form, never saw the popularity that Bentham would have hoped for. It was given limited application, chiefly in hospitals and prisons. And it did not work out to be as perfectly effective in the subjugation of persons as had been proposed.

However, according to Foucault, the idea that it was possible and desirable to achieve social control through the anonymous and automatic operation of power survived and was embraced. The actual technology of power for the objectification of persons and their bodies, as proposed in the Panopticon, was globally installed in the service of the economy. "Administering the accumulation of men was necessary for the accumulation of capital, for the economic takeoff in the West" (1979, p. 168). This technology made the rise of capitalism possible, as it did the disciplines of the human sciences.

> ... the disciplines characterize, classify, specialize; they distribute along a scale, around a norm, hierarchize individuals in relation to one another, and if necessary, disqualify and invalidate. (1979, p. 223)

---

*This is not to suggest that all were equal in their experience of the effects of this power.

Foucault argues that we have entered "the age of infinite examination and of compulsory objectification," that we now have a society of normalization in which evaluation has replaced torture and has infiltrated the judiciary in matters of social control—in the control of bodies, of groups, and of knowledge. This is a form of power that is on the "underside" of the law, one that has infiltrated judicial processes. Foucault refers to the normalization of the law: "reference to statistical measures and judgements about what is normal rather than about what is right and wrong" and "isolation of anomalies and normalization of anomalies through corrective measures" (1979).

SOME FINAL THOUGHTS

I have described some practices associated with the externalizing of problems. These practices have been taken up by a number of other therapists and creatively applied to a wide range of presenting problems in a variety of contexts (e.g., Durrant, 1985, 1989; Epston, 1989).

I have argued that the practices associated with the externalizing of problems may be considered counter-practices to cultural practices that are objectifying of persons and of their bodies. These counter-practices open space for persons to re-author or constitute themselves, each other, and their relationships, according to alternative stories or knowledges. As such, I believe that these practices provide a basis upon which to realize Foucault's proposal that we engage in action to:

> ... liberate us both from the state and from the type of individualization which is linked to the state. We have to promote new forms of subjectivity through refusal of this kind of individuality which has been imposed on us for several centuries. (1982, p. 216)

In describing certain practices that have been experienced as enabling by persons who have sought therapy for problems, I am not proposing that recourse be made to these practices for all persons, in all situations, and at all times. For example, there are those who seek therapy in relation to various crises, and whose lives and relationships are not fixed by problem-dominated stories. Under these circumstances, it might be appropriate for the therapist to assist the persons to address various aspects of their experience of the crisis, and to review their handling of it.

Then there are those seeking therapy who have accounts of their life that are not problem-saturated, but ones that they regard as rather mundane. Under these circumstances, it could be appropriate for the therapist to encourage persons to identify the "sparkling facts" of their career in life, including those that relate to various turning points, and invite performances of meaning in relation to these. This would have the effect of establishing such "facts" as more significant and would assist the persons to render the account of their lives more unique.

And there are persons who are endeavoring to situate their lives in preferred stories and to embrace alternative knowledges, but who are finding it difficult to do so because of the dominant and disqualifying stories or knowledges that others have about them and their relationships. In these circumstances, it could be appropriate for the therapist to encourage the recounting and the full appreciation of the persons' history of struggle, and to explore possibilities for establishing the conditions that might facilitate performance and circulation of their preferred stories and knowledges.

3. A Storied Therapy

We believe that the appropriateness of applying the logico-scientific mode of thought and the production of scientistic theories in the domain of the human sciences, particularly in relation to social organization, should always be seriously questioned and challenged. To this end, it is helpful to draw distinctions around that mode of thought that gives rise to scientism and that which we believe appropriate in the interpretation of events in human systems.

This very distinction is drawn by Jerome Bruner (1986). He contrasts the logico-scientific and the "narrative" modes of thought.

> There are two modes of cognitive functioning, two modes of thought, each providing distinctive ways of ordering experience, of constructing reality. . . . A good story and a well-formed argument are different natural kinds. Both can be used as means for convincing another. Yet what they convince of is fundamentally different: arguments convince one of their truth, stories of their lifelikeness. The one verifies by eventual appeal to procedures for establishing formal and empirical truth. The other establishes not truth but verisimilitude. (p. 11)

Thus, the activity that is informed by the logico-scientific mode of thought is very different from that activity informed by the narrative mode of thought. And the criteria for establishing a good logical argument and for establishing a good story are incommensurable.

The logico-scientific mode of thought involves procedures and conventions that warrant it as a legitimate endeavor within the scientific community, procedures and conventions that prescribe the application of "formal logic," "tight analysis," "empirical discovery guided by reasoned hypotheses," the production of universal rather than particular "truth conditions," and a theory that is "testably right." The indicative mood provides the context for this endeavor, in that the paradigmatic or logico-scientific mode of thought:

> ... attempts to fulfill the ideal of formal, mathematical system of description and explanation. It employs categorization or conceptualization and the operations by which categories are established, instantiated, idealized, and related one to the other to form a system. ... At a gross level, the logico-scientific mode ... deals in general causes, and in their establishment, and makes use of procedures to assure verifiable reference and to test for empirical truth. Its language is regulated by requirements of consistency and noncontradiction. (Bruner, 1986, pp. 12–13)

The narrative mode of thought, on the other hand, is characterized by good stories that gain credence through their lifelikeness. They are not concerned with procedures and conventions for the generation of abstract and general theories but with the particulars of experience. They do not establish universal truth conditions but a connectedness of events across time. The narrative mode leads, not to certainties, but to varying perspectives. In this world of narrative, the subjunctive mood prevails rather than the indicative mood.

Jerome Bruner (1986), when inquiring into what makes a story a good story, into what constitutes a story of literary merit, refers to the presence of certain mechanisms that render the text indeterminate and that recruit or enlist the reader "in the performance of meaning under the guidance of the text," so that the text becomes a virtual text in relation to the actual. These mechanisms are those that "subjunctivize" reality, and he describes three of them:

The first is the triggering of *presupposition*, the creation of implicit rather than explicit meanings. For with explicitness, the reader's degrees of interpretive freedom are annulled. . . . The second is what I shall call *subjectification*: the depiction of reality not through an omniscient eye that views a timeless reality, but through the filter of consciousness of protagonists in the story. . . . The third is *multiple perspective*: beholding the world not univocally but simultaneously through a set of prisms each of which catches some part of it. . . . To be in the subjunctive mode is, then, to be trafficking in human possibilities rather than in settled certainties.

Other authors from other fields of study have also emphasized the importance of the subjunctivizing of reality in the creation of the context for transformations or new possibilities, and thus in the performance of new meanings. For example, Victor Turner (1986) associates the subjunctive mood with the liminal or betwixt and between stage of that class of ritual called a rite of passage.

I sometimes talk about the liminal phase being dominantly in the subjunctive mood of culture, the mood of maybe, might be, as if, hypothesis, fantasy, conjecture, desire—depending on which of the trinity of cognition, affect, and conation is situationally dominant. (p. 43)

Although Jerome Bruner's comments on narrative relate to the structure of texts of literary merit, we believe that persons generally ascribe meaning to their lives by plotting their experience into stories, and that these stories shape their lives and relationships. We also contend that most conversations, including those conversations with the "self," are shaped by at least the rudimentary requirements of a story—they have a beginning, a turn of events and an ending. Thus, narrative is not constrained to literary texts.

Our lives are ceaselessly intertwined with narrative, with the stories we tell and hear told, those we dream or imagine or would like to tell, all of which are reworked in the story of our own lives that we narrate to ourselves in an episodic, sometimes semi-conscious, but virtually uninterrupted monologue. We live immersed in narrative, recounting and reassessing the meaning of our past actions, anticipating the outcome of our future projects, situating ourselves at the intersection of several stories not yet completed. (Brooks, 1984, p. 3)

DISTINCTIONS BETWEEN LOGICO-SCIENTIFIC AND NARRATIVE MODES

In the following discussion, the distinctions around the logico-scientific and the narrative modes of thought are drawn out by considering various dimensions.

Experience

In the logico-scientific mode, the particulars of personal experience are eliminated in favor of reified constructs, classes of events, systems of classification and diagnoses.

In contrast to this, the narrative mode of thought privileges the particulars of lived experience. Lived experience is the "vital" consideration, and the links between aspects of lived experience are the generators of meaning.

It is only when we bring into relation with the preoccupying present experience the cumulative results of similar or at least relevant, if not dissimilar, past experiences of similar potency, that the kind of relational structure that we call "meaning" emerges. (Turner, 1986, p. 36)

Time

As the logico-scientific mode of thought concerns itself with the derivation of general laws of nature and the construction of a world of universal facts deemed to be true for all times and in all places, the temporal dimension is excluded. Not only does the temporal dimension have no bearing on the interpretation of events in this world, but these interpretations must be beyond the effects of time; they must "stand the test of time" and demonstrate invariance in order to qualify as worthy or be considered "true."

In contrast to this, temporality is a critical dimension in the narrative mode of thought where stories exist by virtue of the plotting of the unfolding of events through time. This sequencing of events in a linear fashion through time is necessary to the derivation of any "storied sense." Stories have a beginning and an ending, and between these points there is the passage of time.

> This provisory definition immediately shows the plot's connecting function between an event or events and the story. A story is *made out* of events to the extent that plot *makes* events *into* a story. The plot, therefore, places us at the crossing point of temporality and narrativity. (Ricoeur, 1980, p. 171)

Language

The logico-scientific mode centers around linguistic practices that rely upon the indicative mood to reduce uncertainties and complexity. Through these practices there is an attempt to substantiate reality, an attempt to give speakers a sense of substance, materiality, and surety in the world they inhabit.

As consistency and noncontradiction are guiding criteria in the construction of this world, alternative meanings are excluded by univocal word usage, and quantitative descriptions are preferred over qualitative ones. Technical languages are developed to reduce the risks of polysemy; that is, the potential of words to have more than one meaning, and the potential for the meaning of words to be determined by a unique context in which they might be used. The avowed purpose is to ensure the identity of meaning to the end of the "argument."

The narrative mode centers around linguistic practices that rely upon the subjunctive mood to create a world of implicit rather than explicit meanings, to broaden the field of possibilities through the "triggering of presupposition," to install "multiple perspective," and to engage "readers" in unique performances of meaning. These linguistic practices bring an appreciation of complexity and of the subjectivity of experience.

Rather than privileging univocal word use, polysemy is embraced. More than one line of interpretation or reading at any one time is encouraged, and through increasing our linguistic resources, the range of possible realities is broadened. The unique arrangement of ordinary and poetic or picturesque descriptions is encouraged over technical descriptions, and conversation is less purpose-driven and more exploratory.

Personal Agency

The logico-scientific mode represents personhood as a passive arena that is reactive to impersonal forces, drives, impacts, energy transfers, etc. This is implicit within the terms it sets. It assumes, for the sake of inquiry, that some force or forces internal or external to the person are acting upon the person, and that these are what shape and constitute lives. At times, in such scientific inquiry, persons are reduced to high grade automatons.

The narrative mode locates a person as a protagonist or participant in his/her world. This is a world of interpretative acts, a world in which every retelling of a story is a new telling, a world in which persons participate with others in the "re-authoring," and thus in the shaping, of their lives and relationships.

Position of the Observer

The logico-scientific mode of thought excludes the observer from the observed by the imputation of objectivity. The subject is on the "other side" of the observer and, by definition, is the one to be acted upon. The observer is not implicated in the creation of the phenomena that are being observed, and the subject is held to be immune to the effects of this observation. All this serves to position the observer above and beyond the subject.

The narrative mode redefines the relationship between the observer and subject. Both "observer" and "subject" are placed in the "scientific" story being performed, in which the observer has been accorded the role of the privileged author in its construction.

When we locate a therapy within the context of the narrative mode of thought, stories about life are considered to have been constructed through "the filter of the consciousness of the protagonists." Thus, the transcendental "we" and the "it" of the subjectified person are replaced by the pronouns "I" and "you" of the personified person.

Practice

A therapy situated within the context of the narrative mode of thought would take a form that:

1. privileges the person's lived experience;
2. encourages a perception of a changing world through the plotting or linking of lived experience through the temporal dimension;
3. invokes the subjunctive mood in the triggering of presuppositions, the establishment of implicit meaning, and in the generation of multiple perspective;
4. encourages polysemy* and the use of ordinary, poetic and picturesque language in the description of experience and in the endeavor to construct new stories;
5. invites a reflexive posture and an appreciation of one's participation in interpretive acts;
6. encourages a sense of authorship and re-authorship of one's life and relationships in the telling and retelling of one's story;
7. acknowledges that stories are co-produced and endeavors to establish conditions under which the "subject" becomes the privileged author;
8. consistently inserts pronouns "I" and "you" in the description of events.

---

*Gianfranco Cecchin (1987), in referring to Systemic Therapy, proposes a "polyphonic orientation" and the encouragement of "multiplicity".

The following material reflects our exploration of narrative means within the context of a therapy of this form—a storied therapy.

LETTERS OF INVITATION

Letters of invitation are commonplace in the everyday world so really need no introduction. However, such letters must appear "strange" in the context of the professional-client relationship, which customarily depends on the client's applying for an appointment and being allocated a time. I (D. E.) use letters of invitation when I believe that it is important to engage persons in therapy who are reluctant to attend.

Sally*

Six weeks after her husband's suicide, Mrs. Jones started to roam in the middle of the night in a trance state, accompanied by her 12-year-old grandson. She would tell her neighbor that she was seeking sanctuary for her grandson, whom she believed to be her daughters, from the sexual abuses of her husband. Her daughters, Sally (aged 30 years), Margy (aged 27 years), and Joan (aged 25 years), all lived away from home. Mrs. Jones referred herself to a Community Psychiatric Service, where she was gradually assisted to "remember" and make some sense of a 30-year-long nightmare of sexual torture. A short hospital admission was of some assistance to her in this process.

Margy and Joan, three years previously, had confided in each other about their father's abuse of them. They became exceedingly alarmed and incensed as one revelation led to another. Apart from their own distress, they were also concerned about the abuse of Joan's daughters, aged seven years and four years. The extended family was referred to Leslie Centre in order to assess the abuse of the granddaughters and to assist this family in reconstructing its

---

*The therapists were David Epston and Eileen Swan, Leslie Centre, Auckland.

history. The 12-year-old grandson, who was conceived by father-daughter rape (of Sally), had already been removed from his grandmother's home and placed with Joan. Sally had an extensive psychiatric history and was considered incapable of looking after him. At times, she believed she was possessed by a devil.

We met with Mrs. Jones, Margy, Joan, and Joan's husband, Barry. Great concern was expressed by everyone with regard to Sally's absence and over her adamant refusal ever to attend another "psychiatric place" again. It seemed important to us and her family that Sally participate in the family's reconstruction of events, especially in relation to the placement of her son. The family also felt that some decision should be reached about informing this young man of his parentage. Eileen led the discussion while I drafted the following letter. I then read it, paragraph by paragraph, for discussion and agreement.

Dear Sally,

We all met at Leslie Centre and we were very much aware that you weren't here. We got to talking about you so much that we decided to write you. For all of us, there are pieces of our lives to be puzzled over and fitted together so that our lives make sense to us and we can tell the difference between justice and injustice, love and torture, and the lies that were told to us and the truth that is now evident. Margy and Joan are indebted most to you because they now fully realize that to some extent you sacrificed yourself to save us. You taught us how to hide, how to protect ourselves, and how to run away. You bore the brunt of our family's oppression. Everyone loves you and respects you and admires you for what you have done for others. We now wish to turn the tables on you and do for you what you did for us.

In the past, no-one believed you and, really we weren't able to believe ourselves. Three years ago, Margy and Joan dared to speak the truth to each other and ever since then our lives are painfully fitting together and the confusion and craziness are clearing up.

We have come together as sisters with love and understanding for each other and we would like you to join us. There is a very big hole in our sisterhood when you aren't with us. All that you gave us in the past we should like to give back to you now because you suffered the most and were most tortured.

All of us have been deceived, so our father could perpetrate his violence and sexual tortures against all of us. We were all victims and we are all now survivors. The next step is to set things right for all of us as individuals and to bear witness against the oppression by men of women and girls. We know this is not going to be easy — and that it's going to take time — but we are determined to see it through. We very much want you to be there with us so you can reclaim your self too.

As a family, we have been an occupied zone, invaded and terrorized by our father-oppressor. But now we can and will recapture ourselves, our bodies, our dignity, and our pride. The best way to fight back is as a family because we have not spent all our strength. You did most of the fighting over the bad times and perhaps were most weakened by it. We now would like to give you back some of our strength, because we have more than enough. It is because of you we have become strong, the strong women we are, and we owe you a great debt. You have fought on your own for so long — now we will all fight back together.

Yours with great love,

Sally attended the next meeting, and when the letter was again read, we all cried together.

Haare

Haare was a 13-year-old Maori boy who had been "adopted" by his grandparents at birth. He was the son of their daughter. Such adoptions are sanctioned by Maori custom. Haare's grandmother, and then grandfather, died. Around this period, Haare's asthma became unmanageable. His birth mother was recalled from another city to attend to his care. As he had been reared by his grandparents, she'd had little contact with him, felt she did not know him, and had no parenting authority. Over the next nine months, Haare had six hospital admissions, with one cyanotic attack and two life-threatening attacks. His compliance with medication was poor, and his cooperation was nil; in fact he refused to speak on most clinic visits. On his most recent respiratory arrest, he was delivered to the accident and emergency department over the crossbar of a friend's bicycle. His medical consultant expected him to perish in the near future and gave me permission to make this known to the family. His birth mother attended one meeting at my workplace along with Haare. Haare refused to speak with me and his mother seemed humiliated and flummoxed by the situation. All the subsequent appointments were not attended, despite my frequent telephone calls.

In response, I wrote the following letter to Haare's mother:

I would prefer to meet with you and those who are concerned about the fact that Haare doesn't care for his body instead of attending his tangi* and grieving over his body.

I feel so worried that, if you choose not to have a meeting, please ring me and tell me that you think I have done everything possible to stop Haare's dying.

Yours sincerely,
D. E.'

Haare's mother rang within days requesting a meeting. I insisted that she convene his whanau (extended family) and said that I would not come unless there were at least 20 people in attendance. This was a culturally consistent approach to such a crisis. At this meeting, all agreed on the following formulation that "this boy doesn't care enough for himself and for this reason he may die." Haare, as usual, ignored all those gathered at his home. Haare had also not attended school since the death of his grandmother. There was some debate about where Haare should live and who should "mother" him. There was agreement that Haare should remain with his birth mother, although everyone acknowledged that she did not know him very well. All expressed concern that

*Maori word for 'funeral'

she couldn't control him, partly as a result of the overindulgent and overweening care of his now deceased grandparents.

A number of decisions were consensually reached. An uncle was to ensure Haare's regular school attendance. Several of his "aunties" observed that he had never grieved for his grandparents, saying that "his feelings were turning sour inside of him." They thought that they would review photographs and their memories of the grandparents so as to experience their sadness in Haare's presence. His birth mother was sanctioned in her attempt to gain parental control over him, with the proviso that she should call on any of her relatives if need arose. Haare's "cousins" agreed to forbid him to accompany them on their evenings "on the town" if Haare failed to attend school that day.

Following this meeting, Haare had a period of 12 months with only one day in the hospital and, over the next five years, an average of two days per year.

Mrs. Smith *

Mrs. Smith phoned Leslie Centre in early February, requesting help for the family. She was very anxious about her elder daughter, Jane (aged 15½ years), whom she described as having a very poor self-image, being in conflict with her mother, aggressive towards other family members, and not attending school. An appointment was made for six weeks later. At this stage we knew little more than the above information, plus the fact that this was a two-parent family with two daughters. The other daughter was nine years old.

The appointment time came, but the family did not appear. About 15 minutes later, there came a desperate phone call from Mrs. Smith, who felt everything was hopeless. Jane had refused to come to the appointment and there had been a big family row. On further questioning, we found that, among other things, Jane was refusing to leave the house because she had a particularly bad outbreak of acne. At the end of our conversation it was agreed that

*Co-authored by Mary Underwood (Leslie Centre) and David Epston.

we would meet with or without Jane in two weeks' time. In the meantime, we would send a letter to Jane.

We composed the following letter:

Dear Jane,

I'm writing because we didn't get to meet each other last Wednesday at 5 p.m.

My name is Mary. I've worked at Leslie Centre for four years. I have a daughter just a little younger than you.

When your mother phoned to say your family wouldn't be coming in, she said you were feeling badly with acne that had flared up. I can understand how you felt—I sometimes get a rash on my face and neck myself.

It's hard writing to you when I don't even know what you look like. If you send me a photo, I'll send you one.

Well it's pretty clear that things are going wrong in your family. Growing up is very hard these days—I'm sure it's harder than it used to be. It sounds like you're failing to get to school sometimes and failing to get on with your life. That would sure make anyone feel miserable.

When I meet with your mother and father next time, I would think that you'll probably have another attack of acne—and I know what it's like to face people when you're not at your best—I do it quite often.

So I'll understand if you don't feel up to coming and facing into your future.

But, on the other hand, I'd feel really badly talking behind your back with your mother and father.

I've been thinking of this dilemma quite a bit and I've come up with some ideas. I wonder what you think about them:

1. *Could you get a friend to represent you at the session—a bit like a lawyer—who could come in your place and speak for you?*
2. *If that's not a good idea, what about you let your mother or father choose a friend of theirs to represent you?*
3. *If that's not a good idea, what about you go on "stand by"*

*at the telephone while your parents are here? Then I can
call you if I get the impression that your parents have
forgotten what it's like to be your age. I can ask for a few
ideas about how it feels for you.*

Sounds like you've got your parents pretty worried about you.
*If you really want to show your parents this letter it doesn't
really matter. But I'd prefer you didn't.*
*I'm planning to meet with your mother and father on Wednes-
day, April 3rd, at 5:30 p.m. I suppose you might come or you might
not or you might try one of those other ideas. It's up to you, I
guess.*
Well, bye for now,

> *Yours sincerely,*
> *Mary*

The whole family came to the next appointment. Jane became
firmly engaged in the discussion. We had two sessions with the
whole family and two sessions with the parents.

At follow-up a year after the initial contact, Jane was regularly
attending school and was going out with a boyfriend but within
limits set by her parents. Conflicts between Jane and her parents
were now described as "nothing like what we had before" and "just
normal."

REDUNDANCY LETTERS

I (D. E.) have contributed to many letters that make people
redundant in such roles as "parent-watcher," "parents' marriage
counselor," "brother's father," etc. Following is a small sample of
such letters.

Charlotte and Danny

Charlotte, who had been addicted to heroin for nine years,
wished to resume her position as "mother" to her son Danny, 12
years old. This had caused considerable difficulties between her
and Danny. Charlotte was desperate to become her son's mother;

Danny was just as desperate that he remain his mother's father. We requested that Charlotte write Danny a redundancy letter, since she no longer required his "fathering." She waited until the next session to read it to him. Tears rolled down Danny's cheeks as Charlotte requested that they exchange roles.

Dear Danny,

I am writing this letter thanking you for your services over the past eight years of your life. Services which included looking after me when I was sick. Watching over me and your sister. Now while I think of it, you never moaned even though everything I did was selfish. You became the mother, father, housewife, cook, and cleaner, whenever I failed.

You sacrificed your childhood in order to make our lives easier to live.

You were strong when I was weak. You learned to cope with sorrow and pain at a young age where all I learned was to smother and bury them.

Your service was far beyond excellence in the way that you counseled me through those years — without being demanding. You made me see and accept what I was doing to us by confronting me.

You nursed me when I was sick and encouraged me when I gave up. Never deserting your position. When I lost sight of my direction, you showed me the way.

Now that I am well, there is only one way I can thank you for everything you have done, and that is to let me be to you what you were to me.

Thank you for being my counselor and please be happy that you are relieved from all your services in the past with the highest recommendation.

Mary and Tom

Mary (aged 24) and her younger brother Tom (aged 16) were locked in a struggle over authority. Mary felt she should have authority over Tom, whereas Tom felt he should have authority over himself. The second session was taken up with helping Tom prepare his discharge letter. Here is Tom's letter:

I, Tom Jones, discharge my sister, Mary, from being like a mother to me. This may have been necessary when I was much younger but it is no longer the case. I have come to realize how worried you are about my success in life and this has probably been going on inside of you for some time now. As a result, you have come to feel responsible for me and guilty when you don't feel like putting yourself out for me. You took on this role when I was young and needed looking after. You have done such a good job on me that you can now step aside and let me try my wings. I do not want to be your puppet so both of us are going to have to cut some strings.

I have decided against violence by having my mother agree to charge me with assault if I strike you again. Until we get used to being equal as brother and sister, it is very likely we will still have arguments, with each of us trying to have the last word. Instead of that, I suggest we put these matters of disagreement to a coin toss. In this way, we both will get used to winning 50% of the time and losing 50% of the time. In this way, we both will be equal. I now will not have to prove to you that you are not my superior and I am not your inferior. We are equal and, by being equal, we have a chance to become brother and sister instead of "son" and "mother."

I thank you for what you have done for me when I was young. I think all the caring you did has given you a lot of practice for becoming a nurse.

Signed by: _____
on the _____ day of _____ 1986
Witnessed by (mother): _____

Mary thought about this and came to the conclusion that she should discharge herself:

I, Mary Jones, have served my brother well over the years when he required my attentions. As he has grown older, he has required my supervision less, although I have continued to worry about him. I had become convinced, because of his violence towards me, that he required more of my supervision. I have become in danger of having a bond turn into bondage. My brother, by discharging me from acting like his mother, is asking that I cut the strings because he doesn't want to be my puppet and because he wants me to give him a chance to stand on his own two feet. He says, along with my mother, that passing or failing his School Certificate examinations is his problem, not mine. Both Tom and my mother assure me that, no matter what, he can look after himself and will create his own future.

Both my mother and brother request that I start being more for myself and less for others. They do not wish me to become a selfless, dutiful daughter. Although my mother has never lived on her own, she is noble enough to suggest that I make my own way in life before it passes me by. Being a slave to duty is still a slave, no matter how you look at it.

I also know that my retirement from my role of being like a mother to my brother isn't going to be easy, as I have been doing it all my life.

I should taper off slowly over the next four months. Over this time, I know I shall be torn between duty and becoming a more self-full person. When duty is pulling at me, I may consider being "self-full" selfish. And here I will have my encounter with guilt. David Epston has suggested that I do not confront it head on, but rather spy on its ways and means. David Epston advises against open warfare and suggests reconnaissance missions. Right now, I should only win if I cannot lose.

I am fully aware that David Epston believes that I have done as much as any good parent could do and it is now time for me to graduate Tom. I know too that David Epston hopes this letter will make an impact upon me, although it is unlikely that this will occur in my first reading of the above. I suspect that he thinks that unconsciously I have chosen my nursing training as a way of continuing my caring lifestyle and that I am already ahead of some of my colleagues who have not had my years of training.

Once my retirement is completed, my brother and I will have a chance to form a brother-sister relationship. It is too early yet to *know how that will proceed. I will have to be on my guard as he will still try to solicit the advantages of me being like a mother to him at the same time as resenting it bitterly.*

Signed by: _____
on the _____ *day of* _____ *1986*
Witnessed by (mother): _____

A year later, Mary and I were meeting together again. We were discussing the letters and she recounted a very recent incident:

Once I was sitting on the beach and I got it out (her retirement letter). Just reading it, I stopped crying. I had found out that Tom had lost another job. I went through the things of cutting myself, smashing my head against the wall in the shower because I didn't know what to do. . . . I made myself sick. I found out from my sister and mother that they were going to tell him off. My mother was getting stomach pains. I left and went to the beach and sat down there for ages and ages. I didn't realize I felt responsible until after I read the letter. It was funny . . . it was more my reaction to it. I just stopped crying—it made me feel better. So I looked at the contents of the letter—what was it about? I wasn't responsible for Tom. The letter had served its purpose before, and then I put it in a side of my mind, thinking that its purpose had been served so it could be forgotten.

LETTERS OF PREDICTION

Often, at the end of therapy I (D. E.) ask permission to make my predictions for a person's, relationship's, or family's future. I regularly use the period of six months as my time-frame. I often refer to this time-frame as "your immediate future." I post these predictions in "letters," folded and stapled, with "private and confidential" prominently displayed on them, along with "Not to be viewed until _____ (date in six months' time)." My intentions in doing this are twofold:

1. The prediction proposes a six-month follow-up/review, and suggests that this would be an interesting exercise for both the person/family and therapist to undertake; and

2. Since it is my suspicion that most people won't wait but will review their review prior to the specified date, then I expect that the prediction will function as a prophesy which may fulfill itself.

Alice

Alice, aged 16, was referred by her mother because of her reluctance to work, her involvement with a motorcycle gang and its criminal activities, and the increasing number of tattoos on her body.

Alice had had an unfortunate school career and had "played dumb." She had then been sent to a special school where she gained a strong sense of self along with street wisdom. We met five times, during which Alice started taking herself seriously and decided to return to night school. Her mother was able to become less preoccupied with her daughter and more occupied with her own life. Here is my letter of prediction:

The following is a prediction for the immediate future of Alice Brown, _____ (address). The above mentioned can be aware of the contents of this prediction six months from today on June 15, 1988, or at any time after that date.

My prediction is as follows: Alice will continue to take the new direction she has started out on in the last six months. As time goes by, she will feel less inclined to fake unintelligence and will more and more accept her intelligence and, by doing so, accept herself. To some extent, she has been living a lie told to her by some unhelpful teachers some years ago, but truth will win out. Jane will come to experience in many unspecified ways that the truth about herself and her capabilities is preferable to the lies she has been telling herself and, by doing so, will convince others. There will be a period of transition near the end of this prediction period like the story of the ugly duckling turning into an elegent swan. There may be people in her life who would have preferred her to remain as she was and there will very likely be some uneasiness between these people and Jane. And, as Jane emerges from the shadows, she will make a far stronger appearance in her own life and depend far less on others to appear on her behalf. She will start to take pride in her own accomplishments, as well as pride in others' accomplishments. At almost the very end of this prediction period, she will renounce the idea to one and all that she is unintelligent, and feel a sense of injustice that she has believed this for so long.

I, David Epston, made this prediction in Auckland, New Zealand, on the 15th day of December, 1987.

Signed,
D. E.

COUNTER-REFERRAL LETTERS

Lenny

Lenny, aged 12 years, was preceded by a one-page letter from his concerned family doctor and a nine-page letter from his concerned mother. Lenny had always been regarded as a "worrier, much like his grandmother" by his mother. Six months previously, Lenny had read a pamphlet about AIDS and become convinced that his recurrent pimples were sinister symptoms. He gradually gave up all his social and sporting contacts, lost interest in his previously absorbing pursuits, lost his appetite, and refused to allow his parents to spend any money on his clothing. Instead, he urged them to save for his funeral expenses. Everyone had become very involved in trying to help, and all were frustrated with the futility of their attempts to reason with Lenny.

After our first meeting together, Lenny became so emboldened that he initiated a blood test with his family doctor and then believed in the outcome of a negative finding. Previously he had refused to accept this approach as a way to settle the issue, as he contended that no-one would tell him the bad news.

A month passed and everyone considered Lenny to be "a totally new person," except Lenny, who wasn't willing to go quite so far. He did concede that he was becoming an *encouraged* person. The next session was spent summarizing his bravery renewal for his application to the Monster-Tamers and Fear-Catchers Association of Australia. We all joined in writing Lenny's counter-referral letter:

Dear Dr. Brown,

re: Lenny, aged 12 years

   I have seen Lenny and his family on three occasions — 12/6/88, 12/21/88, and 2/2/89 — and the following is our summary:
   Lenny has started to believe in himself and consequently is disbelieving his fears. Instead of being a fear-driven person, he has driven his fears pretty much out of his life. Sandra (his mother) reported that "there's not the apprehension in any part of his life that he had for the past six months." She had this to say, too: "He proved he was the wonderful person his mother and father always thought he was." Lenny willingly replied that he was "more wonderful than I was." He has also had a number of bravery victories along the way, including fearless trips to the toilet at night, going to a new school and making a new friend almost in the first day, and conquering a fear of surf skiing over the summer. We all considered his bravery comeback so total that I have nominated him for membership in the Monster-Tamer and Fear-Catching Association of Australia. Should he be successful, he will be entitled to offer help to other children who are bugged by fears. Everyone agreed that happiness had now returned to the James family, whereas before frustration and worry prevailed. Lenny's main tactic in overcoming fears was, as he put it: "Facing fears rather than running from them." And the surprising thing was that when he did this, the fears ran from him.
   Many thanks for referring this remarkable young man. It was a pleasure to have met him and his family.

Yours sincerely,
D. E.

cc: James Family

LETTERS OF REFERENCE

Sam and Susan

Sam and Susan were the parents of twins, Eileen and Richard, aged 12. They consulted me over their concern that Richard wasn't enjoying life to the degree that Eileen was. Eileen, it seemed, was extraordinarily engaging and was involved in a myriad of social activities. Richard, on the other hand, had only two or three friends who joined him in his bedroom, which he had turned into an engineering lab. Here they would spend days discussing and drawing up plans for their inventions. At times, they would progress to prototypical models. Although Richard appreciated his sister's sociability, he, in turn, had dedicated himself to engineering and was determined to pursue this at the university.

Sam and Susan very much admired Eileen's active social life. It turned out that both of them had what they described as "unhappy and lonely childhoods." Despite their very obvious accomplishments in many ventures, they both felt decidedly unaccomplished. They seemed oblivious to my observation that their passionate concern for each other had more than made up for the inadequacies of their respective childhoods. They were taken aback when I (D. E.) gave such considerable weight to the relationships they had constructed (rather than to the families they came from). Richard, who had defended himself ably against his parents' concerns that he was "lonely and unhappy" and that he was repeating his parents' experience of their childhoods, took this opportunity to assert: "The only way they would believe me is if they got a letter from a psychiatrist." I inquired, "Richard, do you think a letter from me will be sufficient?" Both Eileen and Richard agreed that it might. After I discussed it further with Sam and Susan, all consented to "a letter of reference."

To Whom It May Concern:

Sam and Susan Martin, in the opinion of the author, are judged to be extremely good and caring parents. They are impressive in the following ways:

1. Unlike many parents, they have encouraged their children, Eileen and Richard, to have their own opinions and to develop their own courses in life with respect to their differing inclinations and talents. They have provided a family context in which their children are appreciated and, by virtue of this, their children appreciate themselves. Eileen and Richard are starting to grasp who and what they really are and can be.

2. In regard to the twinship of their children, they have found ways to differentiate them and have each twin appreciate the other's differences without envy or undue jealousy. Eileen has developed her social skills, whereas Richard is a very constructive and imaginative young man.

3. They have found ways to promote their children to the extent that, whenever either has to face a problem in life, they do not retreat from it but find ways to confront it. I found Richard and Eileen to very creative problem-solvers.

4. On occasions, Richard and Eileen's disputes reach such a noise level that their parents are invited by such squealing to intervene. I believe this is unnecessary and have advised them as to a possible solution, so that they can decline such invitations for their participation.

5. They are very concerned parents who obviously want experiences for their children very different from their own childhoods. From what I know, they have been extremely successful and, compared to the misery of their childhoods, Eileen and Richard have got it pretty good. Once Sam and Susan accept that they don't have to be perfect parents, Eileen and Richard will be more accepting of their own imperfections. After all, no-one is perfect; nor should they be.

It was a very pleasant experience for me to meet and discuss parenting with such well-informed, thoughtful, and concerned parents. If every child had parents such as these, many of the "ills" we associate with children and adolescents would not exist.

Yours sincerely,
D. E.

P.S. This reference is valid until 9/22/87 (a period of one year). If required, it can be renewed after this date.

Sam and Sally did not require a renewal.

Freddy

I (M. W.) knew that Freddy was mischief from the first moment that I saw him. He came into my room with his mother and siblings and immediately "cased the joint." He had a mischievous grin and electric eyes that darted around the room. Even when sitting he seemed alert and ready for action.

Freddy's mother, Jan, was at her wits' end. Freddy was out of control. He was in trouble, yet again, for breaking into cars and stealing cigarettes, was on the verge of being expelled from school, had terrorized the neighbors to such an extent that one family had felt compelled to move from the community, had recently been caught selling dope, and was entirely uncooperative with other members of the family. All this, and only 10 years old. What could be done?

I questioned family members about the influence of mischief in their lives and relationships, and then about their influence in the life of mischief. Although all agreed that Freddy had nearly lost his life to mischief, there were a couple of examples of occasions when he still had the upper hand, during which he could have submitted to mischief but didn't. The fact that Freddy still had some influence in the life of mischief appealed to him, and he thought that he would like to try to extend his influence. He planned to "pull the rug out from under the feet" of mischief. This idea also appealed to other family members, and they all discussed plans to reclaim their lives and relationships.

Upon their return I was shocked by the extent of Freddy's victory over mischief. So was David Epston, who happened to be visiting me at that time. How were others responding to the news of Freddy's escape from mischief? We discovered that many of those who had witnessed the change had also been shocked; in fact, some had found the news so amazing that they had reacted with disbelief and were still treating him like his old person. After Freddy had been given the opportunity to present details of his victories in high drama, David and I talked about how Freddy might be helped to introduce the new picture of himself to disbelievers, so that they would be encouraged to treat him like his new person. David suggested that a "to whom it may concern letter" might be helpful. Freddy was enthusiastic about the idea, and 20 copies of the following letter were sent to him to distribute to chosen people.

To Whom It May Concern:

As you know, Freddy has been a mischief-maker for some time. He has been up to mischief in the following ways:

> *(a) uncooperative and uncontrollable;*
> *(b) stealing;*
> *(c) smoking;*
> *(d) lying;*
> *(e) terrorizing neighbors;*
> *(f) not concentrating;*
> *(g) not doing school work.*

After our meeting on the July 22nd, Freddy returned one week later and had decided to abandon his mischief lifestyle. I must confess that I was as surprised to hear this as you will be to read it. For that reason I questioned Freddy, his mother, and his brother very closely to see if there was any evidence to support this reported self-transformation. I discovered that Freddy had:

> *(a) changed his feelings and become more sensitive to others, highlighted by his newfound ability to look after others;*
> *(b) stopped smoking;*
> *(c) stopped stealing;*
> *(d) stopped terrorizing neighbors;*
> *(e) been taking sides with cooperation;*
> *(f) been having a victory over his lying;*
> *(g) had a better attitude towards his school work.*

Of course it is too soon for me to pronounce Freddy cured of his mischief lifestyle. I gave Freddy and his family the following advice:

1. *Freddy was to pursue his new direction even though many of his friends and enemies would find it hard to believe that he was a new person and would treat him like his old person.*
2. *His mother and brother were to keep an eye open for any further evidence that Freddy was persisting in his new direction.*
3. *My third piece of advice was that Freddy should deliver this letter to important people in his life like yourself so that they would not be surprised by Freddy's newness and would not treat him according to his old mischief lifestyle.*

Of course, I cannot guarantee that Freddy's new lifestyle will continue. That's up to Freddy.

> *Yours sincerely,*
> *M. W.*

Some months after my last contact with Freddy and his family, I was at a roller-skating rink with my daughter Penny when I nearly came to grief. I was out on the rink when the lights were turned down low for a slow number, and a small person flashed by so close that I was nearly scared out of my wits. Before I had time to recover my composure, it happened again, only this time I got a slight bump in the bargain. I was the oldest person on the rink by 20 years at least and felt conspicuous enough without this assistance. The third time I was ready and grabbed the rascal as he went by. I was thrown off balance and began to topple. The small person steadied me and peered up into my face. He then said; "It's me, Mischief!" With a sudden shock of recognition, I exclaimed, "Freddy!"

We had a good talk, and he told me that he had only been pretending to be back at mischief and that he had really "given it the slip." Thank goodness, I thought, grateful that I hadn't got to experience the real thing! Freddy's parents then verified that he was no longer plagued by mischief. Looking back, it was a wonderful chance meeting, but I hope he takes age into account next time around!

LETTERS FOR SPECIAL OCCASIONS

Ray

Eleven months before I (D. E.) met Ray, aged 15, he was involved in a car accident which cost the lives of his revered older brothers, Brian, 19, and Kerry, 17. While his family lived in the country, he attended an Auckland secondary school, staying with his former neighbors, who were "family" to him. He had become more and more distressed as his family was planning the ceremonial unveiling of his brothers' gravestones. This so concerned his "city family," as well as his family in the country, that they sought help from their family doctor, who referred Ray to me. The following letter summarizes our first meeting:

Dear Ray,

The death of your beloved brothers, Kerry and Brian, would have been a great shock and sadness to you. No wonder, only recently, have you come out of shock and are now experiencing your sadness. You have no need to fear this, as it is easily understandable that your brothers' deaths both upset and saddened you. But remember the law of grief: "Crying on the outside means that you are no longer crying on the inside. And crying on the inside drowns your strength." I would imagine that you have some crying to do but you know now that that is right and proper. And if you didn't, it could only mean that your brothers meant nothing to you, and I know that is surely not so. However, you have many people to turn to if you require calming down: your mother, Mrs. Blair, Angela, and Shane. Each and every one of them has his or her own particular way of doing that: your Mum and Mrs. Blair "talk lovingly" to you; Angela knows how "to cheer me up"; and

Shane and you "talk over the things we all (including Kerry and Brian) used to do."

Now you are over your shock, you may be ready to think about ways to keep your brothers' memories alive. You told me that Brian would want you to be a strong person because strength would contribute to your happiness. And here I imagine Brian meant personal strength rather than physical strength. Brian was a very caring person and particularly protective of you, perhaps because you were the youngest. He was the eldest and a very responsible person. As you put it, he "set an example for us." He was an excellent sportsman in both cricket and rugby. But "just being a big brother" probably was the major accomplishment of his too short life. Kerry, too, had many virtues. He taught you how to enjoy yourself and get the most out of life. Teaching you how to enjoy yourself may have been the major accomplishment of his too short life. You told me that you could keep their memories alive by "carrying on growing up in a manner that would please them." Well, Ray, I guess that that won't be very hard for you to do.

Your brothers' unveiling is in a month's time. An unveiling is a special time to lay to rest your sadness and grief but also a time to think about ways to remember them. I suggest we meet again before then and talk about this.

I want you to know, Ray, that even though you have suffered a great loss in your life, you struck me as a young man who is already almost everything your brothers would have hoped for.

Best wishes,
D. E.

We met again and Ray acknowledged his uneasiness regarding the forthcoming memorial service. Aside from that, he informed me: "I know I'm getting better. . . . Before I thought I'd keep going like this . . . I've felt stronger inside . . . I haven't been getting upset so much . . . not at all . . . only once." By agreement, we set about preparing a "letter" for Ray to read at his brothers' unveiling. This seemed to put his mind at rest:

Dear Ray,

Here is what you might like to "read" to Brian and Kerry at their unveiling over Easter in order to reassure yourself and them that you are keeping their memories alive.

Dear older brothers:

I am keeping your memories alive by doing what you wanted me to do. In cricket, I am doing my best and enjoying it. I presented your Brian and Kerry Johnson Memorial trophy to our school and, what's more, I won the Double Wicket tournament as a junior, along with Matthew, and our names are there with yours. We would have ranked 5th or 6th so we won it against odds. I have already made it as an Auckland rep in Form 2 just like you did, Brian. I'm a big hitter like you were. I want you to know that cricket is both my accomplishment and my pleasure, just as you hoped it would be. So far, I know you'd be pleased with me. If I weren't so modest, I'd tell you the high marks I am getting in school. I am keeping up a close relationship with both our parents, even though they've gone apart. They are still good friends though. Because I hung out with you, I grew up ahead of my time. I want you to know that I have stayed friends with your group of friends and I know you wouldn't mind if I made friends of my own. I know you want me to have heaps of fun with girls and to meet one who treats me as well as I treat her. I am following your advice, Kerry: "not to hurt her feelings," "not to be cheeky," "not to get into trouble," and "not to do anything you wouldn't do." I am following an academic direction, hoping to do something requiring qualifications, like accountancy. I have done really well in accountancy and, in fact, it was my best subject last year. I know you will be satisfied that I am keeping your memories alive by doing what you wanted me to do. That is not to say that I don't miss you both and at times am filled with grief and sadness because I miss you both so much.

Ray, I was glad to hear that you were getting better, knowing that the feelings you have won't go on forever. Knowing this has probably strengthened you. For this reason, you are no longer getting more upset than your understanding permits.

I wish you well at your brothers' unveiling.

D. E.

Ray rang to tell me that the unveiling was a great relief to him, and ever since he had felt really good and didn't need to be "calmed down" anymore. His mother and Mrs. Blair happily concurred with Ray's account of his well-being.

Julie

Julie, aged 26, had been raped, badly assaulted, and had her life threatened by her drunken husband shortly after she left him. She had laid charges, was seeking compensation, and was trying to make herself feel more secure. However, she found that all her friends and family were "putting pressure" on her, and she worried that she was going to lose her mind. Much of the advice was unsolicited and contradictory ("you've got to give him another chance" versus "he must go to jail"). On top of everything else that had happened, she found the confusion unbearable.

By agreement, I (D. E.) provided this "to whom it may concern" letter:

To Whom It May Concern:

Julie has suffered a threat to her life, physical assault, and rape. The consequence for anyone of such an insult to body and mind is called "post traumatic stress disorder." This is the same experience as many injured soldiers have had. Although the immediate suffering is over, unfortunately, the suffering does not stop there. Victims of violence continue to suffer for a long time, even though the bruises might have healed or the cuts scarred over. They suffer in their minds, especially at night when the attacks on them are relived in their nightmarish dreams. By day, they feel full of terror and an overriding sense of fear. They find it difficult to get certain thoughts out of their mind. In their minds they are being beaten and raped, over and over again.

To you, Julie may look like the old Julie, but unfortunately she is not. Even if you asked her, she would find it hard to tell you the agony and terror she is living through everyday, and especially every night. You may find her preoccupied with her thoughts, as if she isn't quite with you. I know you will be able to understand this now. However, you might get the idea that you ought to give her advice or make up her mind for her. I urge you to reconsider such helping. The best way to help is not to pressure her with decisions or force her into anything that she hasn't had the time and energy to think through fully. She has had too much of other people forcing her against her will. And right now she is too weak and vulnerable to protest other people forcing their opinions on her against her will.

If you want to help Julie, give her time and space to heal and recover her mind from terror and the nightmare she lived through. If you feel compelled to give her advice, ask her first if she wants it. Try to give her back her authority in her life, which has been violated. The best thing you might do is ask her how you could be helpful instead of deciding how you will be helpful. Help her get back in control of her life, a life free of terror and nightmares.

It is well-known that how people respond to victims of violence and rape plays a large part in their recovery.

Many thanks for "hearing" this letter.

Julie used this letter on several occasions and found the help she received was the help she desired.

BRIEF LETTERS

Written means to therapeutic ends need not always be extensive, serial, and time-consuming. Short "one off" letters can be invaluable to persons in their struggle to take their lives and relationships away from the problems they find so troublesome.

Many of the persons to whom I (M. W.) send brief letters are relatively socially isolated. These persons have a great deal of difficulty identifying who they are and have a tenuous existence — so tenuous that it always seems at risk. Certainly, their existence as persons of worth is very rarely recognized by others. For these persons, simply receiving mail addressed to them by name constitutes a major acknowledgment of their presence in the world. I have known persons who, so confirming do they find this of their lives, principally validate themselves by carrying with them, at all times, one or two letters that they have received in their own name. When these are the letters that I have sent, I have often been asked to supply fresh copies as the originals have become tattered.

But then, this should be of no surprise. To an extent, mail serves this purpose for most of us. What do most persons first do when they arrive home after being away for a day or so? They go to their mail box. And if persons have been away from their home for a more extended period, they often experience a great imperative to collect the mail before attending to anything else. In part, this can be considered a ritual through which persons reinsert themselves into, and reassert their place in, a familiar world.

The following examples of brief letters are grouped under headings that reflect the various themes addressed in them. However, readers will note a great deal of overlap, and many of the letters could be placed under several of these headings. These letters provide but a small sample of the possibilities for assisting persons in the reauthoring of their lives and relationships through narrative means. And the headings included here do not, by any means, represent an exclusive list of themes that can be addressed through recourse to the text analogy and to Foucault's analysis of power/knowledge.

Post Session Thoughts

Sometimes some of my most interesting thoughts and most important questions occur to me after the end of a session. By asking around, I have determined that this is an affliction shared by a great number of therapists. Of course, we can't know whether these would be as important to the persons with whom we have been meeting as they seem to be to us. However, the feedback that I have received suggests that persons do find it helpful to have these questions before their next meeting.

Some examples of letters that present these thoughts and questions follow.

Dear Marion, Keith, Michelle, and Steven,

After our meeting I was thinking of how I could take your side in your plans to escape from isolation. I decided to take action on this, so I just thought I would write a brief note to ask how your plans are working out. I'll be interested to find out at the next meeting. No need to write back.

See you soon,

M. W.

Dear Rick and Harriet,

I'm sure that you are familiar with the fact that the best ideas have the habit of presenting themselves after the event. So it will come as no surprise to you that I often think of the most important questions after the end of an interview. I sometimes get annoyed that these questions are not more forthcoming and do not present themselves earlier.

Anyway, I thought I would share a couple of important questions that came to me after you left our last meeting:

Rick, how did you decline Helen's* invitations to you to do the reasoning for her? And how do you think this could have the effect of inviting her to reason with herself? Do you think this could help her to become more reasonable?

Harriet, how did you decline Helen's invitations to you to be

*Helen is Rick and Harriet's adolescent daughter.

dependable for her? And how do you think this could have the effect of inviting her to depend upon herself more? Do you think that this could have the effect of helping her to take better care of her life?

What does this decreased vulnerability to Helen's invitations to have her life for her reflect in you both as people?

By the way, what ideas occurred to you after our last meeting?

M. W.

Dear Danny,*

After you left I found myself feeling very thirsty to know even more about how you did it. Did you get yourself into training first?

Now that I have written this I am more than thirsty to know more. In fact I'm very hungry—no, now I'm extremely hungry to know more. If you think of anything that you could tell your Mum and Dad, they could then remind you to tell me the same the next time that we meet. This would help me a lot.

Yours ravenously,
M. W.

Dear June and Peter,

I've just met a couple who reminded me of you. So much so, in fact, that I found myself asking them a couple of the questions that I had asked you. I hope that you don't mind: What is it that you can appreciate about the physical/intimate side of your relationship that does not fit with the Hite Report? and, Dare you acknowledge this?

This couple said they didn't know the answer to these questions, and asked me for suggestions. I said I didn't know what the answer was for them. Do you know yet what it is for you? And, if so, dare you embrace this?

M. W.

---

*Danny had just escaped a longstanding disinterest in food.

Therapist Needs Help

Certain developments in the lives and relationships of persons who have sought therapy defy belief and can leave the therapist floundering, entirely without bearings. On these occasions it is not unreasonable for the therapist to ask for assistance.

The following letters give examples of requests for information about events in persons' lives and relationships, with the express purpose of catching me up on developments, so that I might recover a foothold in the therapy.

Dear Edith, Travis, Darren and Janice,

Look, I don't yet believe that I fully understand exactly what steps you took to take your relationships away from hassles. So I feel left behind and would like you to help me catch up with you.

Hassles had consigned you all to passenger seats in life, and tedium had been grinding down your relationships. Now you are sharing the driver's seat and choosing highways that bring promise of brighter prospects. I would appreciate anything that you can tell me about the mechanisms of this.

Thanks,
M. W.

Dear Grace and Allen,

I think that the dominance of the conflict blinded me to some extent. Thus, I have been caught off balance somewhat by recent events.

Your relationship was a victim to this conflict, but now you no longer seem at its mercy. It did have you into replication, capturing you both in the same old patterns over and over and over and over again. Now you are into origination, and adventure, and this appears to suit your relationship.

Would you be prepared to inspect this transformation in your relationship and fill me in on some details that might assist me to come out of the shadow that the old conflict has cast over the therapy?

Yours sincerely,
M. W.

Nonattendance

At times the persons that families are most concerned about decide not to accompany them to therapy. It is not always essential for the therapist to make contact with these persons, as other family members can undermine the problem by investigating ways of refusing to cooperate with its requirements of them.

However, when these persons who do not attend are finding that the problems are highly restrictive of their lives and contribute to a sense of personal failure, letters that engage them in a performance of meaning around unique outcomes can be beneficial.

Dear Gary,*

Today I met with your Mum and Mrs. Jenkins. They told me that you had turned your back on insecurity and were running out on it. I hadn't expected this so soon, so I thought I had better check some things out myself.

- *Have you really made three friends?*
- *Is it true that you are happier?*
- *Is it so that you are now having your own mind about things, and that you don't need other people to have a mind for you?*
- *Is it possible that you are already talking for yourself and that you don't need other people to talk for you?*

If this is all true, then what's your secret?
I said that I thought that insecurity might try to get the better

---

*Gary had just succeeded at pulling himself free of elective mutism and school refusal.

of you again, but your Mum and Mrs. Jenkins said that if it tried you would probably just outrun it. What do you think?

I know that these are difficult questions, but if you can, answer any of them: Would you be happy to tell your Mum so that she can tell me what they are? Or would you rather tell me yourself? Or would you rather keep the answers to yourself?

> Might see you some time,
> M. W.

Dear Graham,

As you know, I've met with Joyce on a couple of occasions. She has told me that she has been quite concerned for you over some time. I guess that you know this, too.

During our second meeting, several unexpected events came to light and I was interested to know more about them. A couple of these events related to your life, so I told Joyce that I wanted to write to you. She thought that you would not mind if I did.

I understand that you have been very critical of yourself over what you see as your dependence on Joyce. She believes that this dependence has made it difficult for you, at times, to cope with the fact that she has her own life and her own friends. Although you had taken action to stop dependence from suffocating Joyce's life, until recently it appears that it has continued to haunt your life.

The unexpected events that I am referring to suggest that you have now taken action to shrug off dependency. It appears that you are not hanging out with the old past so much, and that you have traded an indirect life for a direct life. I am sure that Joyce would be happy to give you the details of the unexpected developments that we have discussed.

I would like to know what happened that helped you to loosen the grip of dependency on your life. I would like to know if you are aware of the significance of this for your future. I would like to know what effect this had on your picture of yourself as a person. If you are prepared to consider these questions, would you also be prepared to pass your thoughts on to Joyce so that I might be more fully acquainted with developments?

Yours sincerely,
M. W.

Recruiting an Audience

The endurance of new stories, as well as their elaboration, is enhanced if there is an audience to their performance. There is a dual aspect to this. First, in the act of witnessing such performances, the audience contributes to the writing of new meanings, and this has real effects on the audience's interaction with the story's subjects. Second, when the subjects of the story read the audience's experience of the new performance, either through speculation about these experiences or by a more direct identification, they engage in revisions and extensions of the new story.

Apart from the fact that letters from therapists actually signify an audience, they can be helpful in encouraging persons to recruit a wider audience to the performance of new stories and in inviting persons to enter into an experience of the audience's experience of the new meanings.

Dear Hilary,

After our last meeting I had some further thoughts about your resignation from being responsible for everyone else.

I wondered how your relatives and friends might react to this. Will they be enthusiastic about the fact that you no longer accept invitations to be a taken-for-granted person or will they attempt to continue as if everything is just as it was?

My guess was that some people would find it difficult to relate to your resignation, and instead, through habit, continue to invite you to be dependable for them. And some of these invitations could be difficult to contend with.

If this is a distant possibility, then it might be helpful to others and to yourself to go public on your resignation. Since you have some knowledge of the publishing world, I thought that you might have some ideas about an appropriate "press release."

What do you think of this idea? Which persons do you think would benefit most by being included as part of the audience to this press release? And what, in your opinion, would be the best way of including them?

Yours sincerely,
M. W.

Dear Tony,
You were everyone else's person. You were compelled by what everyone else thought of you. Now you are your own person. Now you do what you identify as fitting for you. But there is much that is not visible to me. Perhaps this is visible to you.

Tell me, if it's all right: What was the turning point for you? What stands out as a particularly crucial realization, and when and where and in what context did this take place? And when did you first observe the effects of this realization in your life and relationships?

Perhaps the other people in your life might be able to help out with some details in response to this last question. Would you be prepared to ask them what they have noticed that is different about you and when they first noticed this? And how this might have affected their picture of you as a person?

If you are interested in taking any notes in relation to these questions, we could discuss them at our next meeting.

Yours sincerely,
M. W.

Mapping of Influence

Persons who have virtually lost their lives to problems find it difficult to escape despair, even when evidence suggests that they have had some success in reclaiming themselves. This despair can make them oblivious to their progress against the claims of the problem and can have the effect of turning back the clock in their lives.

Thus, under these circumstances, it is imperative that persons have, at their disposal, devices that enable them to map their progress in the repossession of their self-territory. One such device requires the assessment of the influence of problems in the lives of persons versus the influence of persons in the lives of problems. This establishes the relative influence of persons and problems, and can be expressed in a percentage. The installation of such devices can be encouraged through recourse to letters.

Dear Molly,

Anorexia nervosa had claimed 99% of your life. You only held 1% of your own territory. You have said that you now hold 25% of your own territory. This means that you have reclaimed 24% of yourself from anorexia nervosa, and you achieved this over the last eight months. And yet, you despair for all those lost years, for the two-thirds of your life under its influence.

Tell me, if you were to pick up another 24% over the next eight months, and then 24% over the next eight months and so on, how long would it take you to reach 200% and be experiencing double value in your life? And should you keep on in this way, how old would you be at the point when you have regained all the time that was lost? And what will it mean that your life is accelerating right at the time that others are slowing down in their lives?

Just curious,
M. W.

Dear Clive, Lori and Virginia,

You all believed that conflict had overpowered your lives. You felt that your relationships were entirely victims to conflict. Despite your intentions to the contrary, it seems that it always so easily caught you in its web, and you felt compelled to replicate the same old tired and worn-out responses to each other.

However, at our meeting, it was discovered that conflict only had 85% control of your lives, and that you were not entirely at its mercy. You worked out some ideas to extend your own influence, with the plan of eventually having your lives to yourselves.

Since our meeting, to what extent do you think that you have weakened the grip of conflict on your relationships? This might not be easy for you to determine. Conflict is rather blinding, and could make it difficult for you to identify any of the small but significant changes that you might have already initiated. Extreme thoughts, like the idea that it is possible to immediately wrench one's life and relationships free of conflict, also tend to blind persons to changes.

Perhaps, at your next "escape from conflict" meeting, you could review the extent to which you have freed your lives and relationships. Don't forget, you already had 25%.

Yours sincerely,
M. W.

Historicizing

The historicization of unique outcomes often enables persons to locate and embrace their own unique story of struggle, and to identify alternatives to those "unitary" knowledges through which their lives and relationships have been constituted. The identification of these alternative knowledges helps persons to defy those specifications of the unitary knowledges and to form lives and relationships according to knowledges that are more encapsulating of vital aspects of their lived experience.

Letters can play an instrumental part in encouraging persons in the location of their unique histories of struggle, and in the identification of alternative knowledges.

Dear Tammy and Wes,

You left me with some important questions. Or should I say that, after you left, some important questions presented themselves to me? This so often happens after an interview.

In regard to this wisdom that you are now bringing to bear in your approach to parenting and to your relationship, what is its history? I had the sense that you were bringing something forward from "way back."

Does this wisdom have a tradition? If so, have you done some specific remembering that has enabled you to bring alive this special knowledge? What did you do to jolt your memories?

One last question. Were you also presented with interesting thoughts after our last meeting that might assist you to carry this tradition further forward?

I look forward to catching up with you again.

M. W.

Dear Jenny,

I think that we are all witnessing a rupture in your history of self-rejection. At our recent meeting in trying to understand what this rupture was all about, all evidence suggested that it appeared to mark a transition in your life from self-erasing to self-embracing.

The information that you gave clarified for me that there was a pioneering dimension to this, in that those who had gone before you had lives that were history driven.

In the light of this, I was left with further questions that I thought I would commit to paper.

- *What was the history of your struggle that led to this rupture?*
- *Are there traces of similar struggles that might be identified in the lives of those who went before you?*
- *How could this be assessed?*

If these questions arouse your interest, I would be interested to hear of your responses.

Bye,
M. W.

Challenging the Techniques of Power

Many persons have found letters to be of assistance in boosting their resolve to challenge or protest the operation of the techniques of power in their lives and relationships.

This has been the case when that which the person experiences as problematic is primarily identified in relation to:

1. a subjugation to specific techniques of power that are instituted by others, and/or
2. a participation, as a vehicle for and instrument of power, in the subjugation of others, and/or
3. a subjugation to the techniques of self, in which the person is the instrument of power in his/her own subjugation.

The following letters provide some examples of the possibilities for assisting persons in their protest of the techniques of power.

Dear Jake,

When we were discussing what your problem required of you in order to guarantee its survival, your participation in the application of special techniques for blaming others seemed essential.

So you decided that you would refuse to be an instrument of the problem, went on strike against it, and dismissed these techniques for blaming others from your life.

At a meeting, I mentioned this to some colleagues and they were eager to know how this had affected the attitudes of others towards you. We decided to send you a couple of the questions that we were preoccupied with in our discussion:

> • *How do you think this strike has affected the picture that others have of you as a person?*
> • *What, in turn, has this helped you discover about yourself that you can appreciate?*

I look forward to hearing about what you turn up.

M. W.

Dear Sue,

Bulimia has required a great deal of you. Its survival has been expensive to you.

It has required you to operate upon yourself. It has required you to reject yourself. It has required you to subject yourself to a constant evaluation of your body and your person. It has required docility.

Despite this training, you thought that you were ready to take your life back by exposing bulimia, by putting a friend in touch with your experience of it. Quite a risk! And it worked.

After you left our last meeting I thought of some questions that I would have liked to have asked you. So I decided that I would put them in a letter. I hope that you do not mind my doing so. Please do not feel compelled to consider these questions. And please don't feel under any obligation to answer them.

- What do you think your friend appreciated about you as a person that would not be tolerated under the regime of bulimia?
- What does this tell you about yourself as a person that you would have otherwise been blinded to?
- What sort of knowledge about yourself as a woman is this?
- How does this knowledge, about yourself as a woman, set you apart from the ideas about women that bulimia depends upon for its tyranny?

I know that you believed that you were ready to take another step against bulimia by further protesting secrecy. You are taking on quite a lot. Good luck!

I look forward to catching up with the news at our next meeting.

M. W.

Challenging Specifications for Personhood and for Relationship

Letters that support persons in their challenge of dominant "truths" about personhood and relationship are invariably experienced as enabling. These "truths" are those that are specified by the "unitary and global knowledges," and they are usually identified as subjugating of persons and/or of their relationships.

These letters further encourage persons to perform meaning around those aspects of themselves and/or of their relationships that they can appreciate, but that do not fit with the norms and expectations—in short, the specifications—that are proposed by the unitary knowledges. In this process, persons are actively engaged in the redescription of their lives, and in the establishment of alternative knowledges of personhood and of relationship.

Dear Rex,

At our last family meeting, we discovered that the depression had nearly convinced you that you had failed to become a reasonable person, that you had failed to measure up. It also became apparent that the depression was dependent, for its survival, upon this sense of failure.

We then reviewed the sort of expectations that you had supposedly failed to achieve and discovered the devastating effect that these had been having on your life. You then remarked that you had felt very much pushed around by them. Your parents thought that it could be these very expectations that were supporting the depression.

However, when we looked at your influence in the life of the depression, we were able to identify "one and a half" personal qualities that you could appreciate about yourself, and that did not fit with these expectations.

This aroused everyone's interest, and we were all curious about what this said about you as a person. It certainly told us all that you didn't have to be a person for the expectations. This left us with some unanswered questions.

- *If you were to further appreciate yourself without siding with these expectations, what do you think you might get in touch with?*
- *What other steps could you take to prove to these expectations that you do not intend to turn your life over to them?*
- *Would these steps have the effect of undermining the depression?*

We did have other questions, but you made it clear that you only wanted to take three at a time. I guess your assertiveness about his is another example of your defiance of these expectations.

I look forward to our next meeting.

Yours sincerely,
M. W.

Dear Shelly and Ken,

As agreed, I am writing to you with some comments that relate to our recent meeting.

At that meeting you both, in different ways, shared with me your conclusions about your relationship. You agreed that you had not even come halfway close to having anything that resembled a reasonable relationship.

We discussed the formula for relationship that you had been attempting to apply yourself to, and two things became apparent:

(a) That this was a particularly modern formula, perhaps even a formula of the future.

(b) That you had nearly succeeded in completely submitting your relationship to this formula.

However, we did discover that your relationship had not totally succumbed to a modern formula. For example, it was clear that you didn't feel entirely crushed, shattered and written off by the fact that you don't have simultaneous orgasms. But rather, you had found ways of enjoying aspects of your intimate relationship that didn't fit with a modern formula. We then discovered other aspects of your relationship that you were able to appreciate, that were in defiance of this formula.

You agreed to consider some questions in relation to these discoveries:

• What does this successful resistance to shaping your lives according to a modern formula reflect about your relationship?

- *If this resistance is supported by some other ideas about how relationships can be, what sort of ideas are these? What is the source of these ideas?*
- *Dare you embrace these discoveries about your relationship and extend your protest by siding with these alternative ideas?*

I look forward to hearing your thoughts about these questions.

Yours sincerely,
M. W.

That Reminds Me!

I (M. W.) often meet persons who remind me of other persons, sometimes of those whom I have met in therapy. Also, at times I experience events that remind me of some aspect of the lives and relationships of the persons whom I see in therapy. On certain occasions, I write brief letters to these persons; the following represent a small sample of these.

Dear June,

Today I met a young woman who has been struggling to make an appearance in life. At the end of our meeting she thought she was ready to take a step similar to the one that you thought that you were ready to take.

Since she reminded me of you, I became curious about what you had discovered about your readiness. Have you commenced your comeback to life, or was it too soon for you to take that step? I just thought I would tell you this, as I am sure that my curiosity can wait until our next meeting.

Yours sincerely,
M. W.

Dear Fred,

Are you surprised to get this letter? I'm surprised that I'm sending it. It's just that yesterday I was distracted by a person doing pushups in the park and I tripped over a gutter and stubbed my toe.

What has this got to do with you? Well, at our last meeting, I remember that you had a sore foot. My hurting my toe jolted me into thinking of your foot, and this in turn had me wondering how you are doing. That's all.

See you at the next meeting.

M. W.

Dear Dennis and Fran,

Yesterday, through a series of events, I was reminded of the important and unexpected realizations, about your relationship, that you had presented at our last meeting.

I felt compelled to write and ask what you have noticed about how these realizations have been affecting your relationship since then. Perhaps you wouldn't mind just reflecting back over the last two weeks and making some mental notes to bring with you to the next session.

Yours sincerely,
M. W.

Chance Meetings

It is not at all uncommon for therapists to meet people who are members of the extended family or friendship network of the persons with whom they spend time in therapy. This is particularly the case if the therapist works or consults in an institution like a hospital. Such institutions often involve family members and, at times, friends as well. And for many of the recipients of the services of such institutions, persons met there provide the primary group from which friendships are formed.

Chance meetings of these relatives and friends have often provided the impetus for a letter, particularly when the person concerned is socially isolated. These letters can be very simple.

Dear Ronald,

Just a quick note. I saw your Mum at the hospital the other day. Thought I would write to say hullo and ask how you were getting on.
That's all. Bye for now.

M. W.

Dear Elizabeth,

Candy told me that she had been noticing some big changes in you. But I had to be somewhere else already and didn't get to find out more from her. I would be grateful if you would fill me in.

Regards,
M. W.

Dear Jemma,

I ran into Nick yesterday. I asked after you, but he couldn't tell me much because he has been away working.
So I thought I would send a quick note to say hullo and to inquire more directly as to where you have got to in your personal project.

Regards,
M. W.

LETTERS AS NARRATIVE

Letters constitute a medium rather than a particular genre and as such can be employed for any number of purposes, several of which are demonstrated in this text. In a storied therapy, the letters are used primarily for the purpose of rendering lived experience into a narrative or "story," one that makes sense according to the criteria of coherence and lifelikeness. Accordingly, they are at variance to a considerable degree to those conventions that prescribe both the rhetoric and stylistics of professional letter-writing. By "professional" letters, I am referring to those communications between professionals about persons and their problems. Typically, the persons who are the subjects of these letters are excluded from any access to this record, even though their futures may be shaped by it. In a storied therapy, the letters are a version of that co-constructed reality called therapy and become the shared property of all the parties to it. Letters can be substituted for case records. The person/family is the imagined audience in the creation of these letters; by contrast, some putative professional authority serves as the unseen audience for case recordings. In most cases, such recordings are a conversation with oneself. It is our contention that narrativizing letters more accurately display the "work" than professional accounting methods. Such letters make the therapist accountable in the first instance to the person/family and secondly to their professional community. This is made possible because the letters and the information contained within them are shared, dialogical rather than a professional monologue and, due to their visibility to all parties, can be easily amended, contested, or confirmed. The therapist is also required to co-create a discourse which linguistically includes all or most parties to the conversation at the same time as forsaking a mystifying, exclusive professional code.

Narrativizing practices have some very obvious advantages. Firstly, a person/family's experience is situated in the flow of time. Unlike scientific accounts, narratives make no attempt to eternalize experience; rather, they temporalize it. Bruner argues the necessity for this:

> We seem to have no other way of describing "lived time" save in the form of a narrative. Which is not to say that there are not other temporal forms that can be imposed on the experience of time, but none of them succeeds in capturing the sense of *lived* time: not clock or calendrical time forms, not serial or cyclical orders, not any of these. (Bruner, 1987, p. 12)

Secondly, as stories are richer and more complex than the economy of explanatory schemes, a far wider range of happenings or intentions can be accommodated within them and endowed with meaning. Stories tend to be inclusive and as a result enrich events in people's lives, whereas explanations tend to be exclusive and to ignore those events beyond their purview. Narratives, then, allow for lived experience to be construed in lived time and rendered eventful by being plotted into a story.

A storied therapy, driven by its emplotment, moves forward in time and can generate a certain degree of excitement both for the family and therapist. It is prospective rather than retrospective. All the parties enter into a search for new meanings, new possibilities, which call into question the problem-saturated description or dominant story. Alternative stories either emerge from within the dominant story or are discovered to be running along parallel tracks, but have been suppressed or not admitted onto the record. The alternative story derives from the discovery of "unique outcomes" that are either contradictory to the dominant story or stand as puzzling anomalies. These unique outcomes cannot be plotted into the dominant story. They are either nonsensical or insignificant. Re-authoring involves relocating a person/family's experience in new narratives, such that the previously dominant story becomes obsolete. In the course of these activities, people's own lives, relationships, and relationships to their problems are redescribed. Bruner goes so far as to assert:

> Eventually the culturally shaped cognitive and linguistic processes that guide the self-telling of life narratives achieve a power to structure perceptual experience, to organize memory, to segment and purpose-build the very "events" of a life. In the end, we *become* the autobiographical narratives by which we "tell about" our lives. (1987, p. 15)

Being Even by Getting Even

I (D. E.) had met Ted, aged 17, his parents, his brother, Michael, aged 15, and his sister, Jan, aged 11, a year previously on one occasion. He rang saying that his parents had given him the option of seeing me on his own or having him join them as a family. He admitted that he didn't want to come, but if he had to, he wanted to come alone. I consented to this, and I am glad I did.

Ted told me that, despite his best intentions, he could not withstand his brother and sister's provocations, which included name-
calling and, in the case of Jan, physical violence. It seemed the
more he restrained himself, the less restraint Michael and Jan
exercised in goading him. He admitted that he was particularly
sensitive to the fact that he was not as tall as he desired, and to
losing. Ted was a young man with a success problem—that is, he
was extremely good at just about everything to which he turned
his hand. He found not being wildly successful at every enterprise
hard to accept and perturbing. In particular, not only had his
decision, made some six or seven months back, to create a new
siblingship in his family failed in general, apparently going unno-
ticed by Michael and Jan, but the situation had deteriorated badly.
Ted and I put our heads together, made some sense of recent
events, and co-constructed the course of action outlined in the
summary "letter" I gave him.

Dear Ted,

*It was very enjoyable meeting up with you again. You certainly
have a lot of wisdom for a young man your age.*

*As for your "getting wound up" problem, it could very well be
that you have changed tack in the last six or seven months with
Michael and Jan. You have come to realize that you will be leaving
home in the near future and you are starting to re-value your
brother and sister as important people in your life. Very likely, for
some time now they have been irritations, copy-cat-ists, and com-
petitors. But you always had the advantage of age, experience,
weight, and physical prowess. To some extent, you have dropped
out of the conflict, hoping they would notice and respond differently. To your dismay, quite the opposite has happened. The more
you turn away from your old brother-brother-sister pattern, the
more they turn to it. It's almost as if they are missing your participation and are inviting you back with them by provoking you.
They don't know you want something different. My suggestion is
that you hold a meeting and read or tell them your proposal.*

The proposal is:

1. Tell them that you will be leaving home soon and have come to realize how important they are to you now and how important you intend for them to be in your future.

2. Tell them that you have tried to show them your strong bond for them by not fighting, name-calling, etc., but no-one has noticed it. In fact, it may have had a reverse effect — they have been fighting and name-calling you more lately. You wonder if that is because they think you think you are better than them or above them.

3. Tell them nothing could be further from the truth. Then tell both Michael and Jan absolutely everything you admire about them. And I don't think you are going to have to work very hard coming up with a lot of reasons for your pride in them.

4. Tell them that you wonder if because you were older, bigger, and more experienced, and had these advantages over them for some time (but tell them this is no longer the case), before you can all be equal as brothers and sister, they may need to take some revenge on you so they can **get even with you.**

5. For this reason, you will provide them with a long list of all the ways they could insult you. Include as many references as you can to shortness and losing, e.g., midget, short-ass, Tiny, freak-show, born loser, second rate, hasbeen, second division, etc. This list should be very long, and you will have to search your memory. A copy of the list should be entrusted to Michael and Jan. Also, you might ask Michael and Jan if either of them feels they have to get physical revenge on you. If they do, you might request your parent(s) supervise while they slap your hand so they can feel they are **now even with you.**

6. Tell them, that when you **are all even** (you will know when this is because they will no longer feel they have to get revenge on you), you would like to take them out for dinner. It may be that you will be saying goodbye to them for the meantime, but it is very likely you will be saying hello to a new, even and equal, brother-brother-sister relation-

ship. Perhaps with Jan, you will have to bring up the issue of making your brother-sister relationship nonsexist.

7. *Ted, when Michael and Jan get even with you, remember that this is a lot more than name-calling—it is pioneering an equal and even relationship between siblings.*

Good luck!
D. E.

P.S. If you have any further questions and think I might be helpful, give me a ring (will be away the rest of this week).

Ted rang three weeks later. He was elated and said he wanted to meet again to tell me what had happened. Ted somewhat modified the plan to suit himself: "I said I wanted to get to know them better. They didn't have a response—they thought it was strange. We haven't had a major fight since them. Michael appreciated it more. He started taking my side against Jan—he could see I was trying. That inspired me. I hadn't seen any change before. I can see it now. It's coming about. We are sitting down and talking about it. I'm not reacting." Instead of providing them with "a long list," "I would say—what about this . . . or that? That really put Jan on the back foot. She didn't seem to get a bite out of me. The provocation has gone down by 90% . . . even 95%. It's hardly there. It's gone from black to cream." He had "dropped the idea" of physical revenge. After his forthcoming exams, he proposed "to go to a film with them and go for a meal afterwards." He then went on to tell me that "I feel I should be Michael and Jan's parents as well." Even though his parents, whom he very much admired and respected, remonstrated with him, he felt frustrated that Michael and Jan were so unwilling to accept his advice and counsel. A "letter" once again summarized our meeting.

Dear Ted,

Well, it is clear that your brother-brother-sister problems have disappeared by between 90 and 95% and, as you put it, gone "from black to cream." With such an achievement under your belt, no wonder you say, "I feel so much better about myself."

Still, I would like to challenge you on your feeling that "I should be Jan and Michael's parents as well." Not surprisingly, Jan and Michael "don't listen to me" and you "find it infuriating. . . . I know I could help them. . . . I want to be their big brother." My guess is that, right now, Jan and Michael are not too enthusiastic about that proposal, but more enthusiastic, as the last month has shown, for you to just be their brother, an equal brother.

Now, for some time to come, it is still very likely that you will find yourself "wanting to tell them things" even though you "don't know why I feel that way." Well, I can easily understand why you might feel this way. You have learned a lot so far in your 17 years and some of those learnings have come through paying attention to your mistakes and putting them right. Naturally, being the responsible kind of person you are, you might like to save them from their mistakes by handing over to them your learnings. It looks like Michael and Jan are strong-minded people who would rather learn "by discovery" than through your "instruction." Still, you have something of a giving good advice habit and it may be hard to break.

We arrived at the following solution: You are to read and revise the following letter and make 20 copies of it and give them to Michael. Tell him that you have a "giving good advice" habit which you want to break. See if he will help you with it. Ask him to give you a copy of the letter every time you give him some good advice he would have preferred to do without.

> Dear Michael,
>
> I have always felt like your bigger brother, but now I want us to be equals. But habits die hard. I have been your bigger brother for 15 years now. If you notice me forgetting we are equals and giving you advice you would have rather done without, please give me a copy of this. I have provided you with 20 copies. If you require more, let me know.
>
> > Yours equally,
> > Ted

I wrote a brief note to Ted's parents as they had rung before the first meeting detailing their concerns that their son was manic-depressive and asking if they should seek a psychiatric opinion. They had also rung after our first meeting acknowledging his very obvious improvements.

Dear George and Dorothy,

I am sure that Michael and Jan are both a credit to you, but I would like to draw your attention to my admiration and respect for Ted. Rarely do I meet a young man his age with the same degree of sensitivity to others, self-understanding, and depth. I believe you both have a lot to be proud of in him. The only concern I have for him is his super-responsibility. You might like to think about ways of discouraging him from worrying so much about others, as by doing so he might neglect his own concerns.

Once again, it was a great pleasure speaking with your son.

Yours sincerely,
D. E.

I rang Ted nine months later just as he was on the eve of his departure for overseas. Although he wanted to come and see me and tell me all about it, there wasn't the time. Ted did say, however, that things had worked out just as he had hoped; he was now the equal of his brother and sister.

Backtracking Out of Trouble

Glenn was 13 years old and, by the end of his first year at high school, in trouble. I (D. E.) had met Glenn two years previously in regard to his stealing. His parents reported that after our meeting, instead of solely taking, he had added giving to his repertoire. The next year, he had been "reasonably cooperative," and his parents had so much confidence in him, his sister, aged 16, and his brother, aged 11, that they were able to go out and leave their children at home. Glenn said that he preferred responsibility over irresponsibility, for "if your parents trust you, you feel more safe." However, ever since he commenced high school, Glenn had found himself in more and more trouble. First his school work started slipping;

then he started truanting and hiding out; and finally he was apprehended for shoplifting. This had happened over a period of six months and had caused his parents considerable concern. But, no matter what they did, he wouldn't discuss it and started hiding in his bedroom. His mother sensed "a great big wall, brick by brick . . . " dividing them. Glenn had to agree that getting into trouble was starting to trouble him. According to his mother, he wasn't sleeping well and felt very unhappy.

I sent the following letter to Glenn:

Dear Glenn,

Well, it looks like you have got yourself into trouble. I don't blame you for now wanting to get yourself out of trouble. Your Mum and Dad had really started to trust you last year because you had grown up so much. I too believe you are now grown-up enough to get yourself out of trouble.

The best way to get out of trouble is to figure how you got into trouble. For example, if you are out in the bush and lose your way, the best thing to do is to retrace your steps. So here is a history of your trouble which has started to trouble you.

You breezed through intermediate school without having to do much work. You were able to keep up more or less just by paying attention. Then you took a giant step and moved on to high school. You started there with a burst. Perhaps you thought that, because of that, you could sail through high school. You probably got the idea that schoolwork wasn't worth doing. You also didn't know that no-one would be around to carefully coach and supervise you like your teachers did at intermediate school. You didn't realize that you had to organize yourself rather than having others organize you. No wonder you started to pretend that you were going to school and started failing. It was pretty hard to face up to that so you started hiding behind closed doors and wouldn't discuss matters with your Mum or Dad. "A great big wall grew up between us, brick by brick." In June, you got a part in a musical and this gave you an excuse not to find out what you had missed. So you got further and further behind. You started to really go into retreat now and started skipping school. The school then became alarmed and decided to supervise you by putting you on a "blue card." You then started really giving up on yourself and started shoplifting. Now you were in trouble with the police. The lieutenant from Youth Aid gave you, as you put it, "some good advice," and it seemed to get through to you.

Glenn, your job is to backtrack and get yourself out of trouble. You got yourself **into** it, so it is right and proper to get yourself **out** of it. By doing so you would really impress your Mum and Dad and they would know for sure that you are grown-up because you can learn from your mistakes. This is not to say that you cannot ask your Mum and Dad for help, support, or coaching. But, if you want to pull out of your tailspin, you have to do it. It would be a good idea to keep your Mum and Dad informed of your comeback.

Glenn, it may be that you are not grown-up enough to get **out** of trouble. If so, then your Mum and Dad will have to treat you like a younger person and take over your life more.

I think you can do it yourself, knowing what you now know.

I have included a copy of this letter for Mary and Tom. Please give them a copy.

Why don't we meet together in a month's time so we can find out if you are getting more **into** trouble and become more **troubled**, e.g., unhappy, not sleeping well, etc., **or** if you are getting **out** of trouble and becoming more **untroubled**, e.g., happy, carefree, etc. Ask your Mum or Dad to ring and make an appointment, if it suits them.

Good luck in your comeback,
D. E.

P.S. If you decide to get **out** of trouble, I don't want you to think it will be easy. However, the harder the better. The harder it is, the better person you will become.

We met two months later. The following letter summarized our meeting:

Dear Glenn,

Well, Glenn, instead of getting more **into** trouble, you, as you put it, are getting **out** of trouble. You say you "didn't like being in trouble" and I don't blame you. You are winning back your learning and you say the teachers couldn't help but notice. You are now completing your homework instead of leaving it half done. You are finding tests a lot easier. You are less troubled and are sleeping better, so good in fact that you can't wake up in the mornings. Your mother and father are less irritated and more trusting of you. Your Mum says that she has gone from "−10% to 60–70% trust." Your Dad says he is "a lot more trusting." Your Mum reported that you have "knuckled down to his school work and has a much more mature attitude" to things in general. So it was no surprise to me that you are making new friends.

Glenn, you say you have backtracked out of trouble and "at least got back." Your Dad agrees with you. Your Mum disagrees: "I think he's gone ahead . . . he's dealing with difficulties in a much more mature way . . . he is accepting our limits." Glenn, you say you have tried wildness but it doesn't work. So now you are taming your ambitions. Your mother also noted that you are "much more sensible about his health" in terms of fitness and weight. I gather you are starting to take responsibility for yourself instead of expecting your parents to take responsibility for you. Your Dad also oberved that you are more tolerant towards your younger brother.

Glenn, I am afraid I am going to have to disagree with you and agree with your mother. You have certainly gone ahead; you have not merely backtracked. For if you were the troubled person you were, you could not possibly have done what you have gone and done. For that reason, I urge you to think carefully about what you have done and memorize everything. Some time in the future when you get into trouble, you will be able to recall how you got in and out of trouble instead of becoming a troubled person. Bury these memories but be sure to keep a "map" of where you put them. You may need those memories in your future.

Congratulations on getting out of trouble on the one hand, and going ahead on the other.

Show this letter to Mary and Tom if you wish.

Fond regards,
D. E.

I rang Glenn and his parents six months later. Everyone agreed that he was an untroubled young man. The interesting news was what Glenn had insisted on transferring to another school, even though it was out of zone for him. He told me that it had "more discipline" and that such a regime suited him better. His parents were somewhat disappointed but agreed that he had made a well-considered decision and they respected him for it.

Whatever You Do, Don't Make Me Contact The Police!

Carol had single-parented her five children, now aged between 31 and 16 years, for the past ten years. I (D. E.) had met with Carol, her youngest daughter, and Tony, her youngest child, on three occasions one year previously. The focus was on Tony's physical violence towards his sister. His overt violence quickly abated and, with her mother's express encouragement, Judy (aged 23 years) left home. Throughout this contact Carol has worn a brave front.

This time, things were obviously different. Carol was extremely distraught and told me that in our first meetings "I only gave you crumbs from our table." She now felt she had to confide in somebody. But before she did she looked me in the eye and said, "Whatever you do, don't make me contact the police!" It seemed from her account that, although Tony had refrained from physical violence, he had substituted terror. In addition, he had been convicted of an offence, fined, and had spent a brief period in a boys' home. He still had temper tantrums when Carol wouldn't comply with his requests for money, the use of her car, or the use of her home. He would smash her property and threaten to either cut or kill her or her kittens. She admitted she was frightened for her well-being. She had what I believed to be legitimate concerns that Tony was embarking on a criminal career. She felt helpless to do anything about this.

I externalized and objectified "guilt" and asked Carol a series of complementary questions (White, 1986b). I then provided her with a complementary description of events, which I called "my summary."

"Guilt invites Tony's blaming. Blaming others leads the blamer to accept no responsibility for himself. Guilt-driven people then become super-responsible in the face of their children's irresponsible behavior." She was then provided with some "take-home" questions:

1. How do you understand your vulnerability to guilt? What sort of training(s) have you had in feeling guilty?
2. How do you understand your family tradition of keeping everything within the bounds of the family and feeling that it is disloyal and a betrayal to go beyond the family?

Carol returned a week later. She said that the questions had made sense and then went on to provide a litany of reasons why she should feel guilty. She had felt responsible from the age of five for her father's drinking, and no-one was allowed to know what was going on within their family. In her own family, "we all kept secrets" at the same time. Carol said she was feeling responsible and guilty about each one of her children's trials and tribulations, her deteriorating marriage, and in particular, about Tony's problems.

At the end of this meeting, I gave her two more questions to take home:

1. What are all the reasons I think I should feel guilty?
2. Have I suffered enough yet or do I need to torture myself more?

I was not surprised when Carol came to the next meeting with a very long list of reasons for feeling guilty. The following letter is a summary of that meeting.

Dear Carol,

Your questions were:

1. What are all the reasons I think I should feel guilty?
2. Have I suffered enough yet or do I need to torture myself more?

Your list is as follows:

1. *Looking after another boy when Tony was a preschooler.*
2. *Maybe I haven't loved him enough.*
3. *Leaving Tauranga when Tony was happy at school and shifting to Auckland where school was bad for him.*
4. *Doing nursing training in Tauranga.*
5. *Not makng the marriage work properly.*
6. *Not having anything in common with Tony, even when he was little.*
7. *When Tony was six weeks old my father died. My mother joined me and I gave her the baby after I breast fed him so she could have some comfort and take her mind off her husband's death.*
8. *Showing and saying I don't like the kind of person he has become.*
9. *Maybe giving him double messages.*
10. *Sometimes I feel like giving up and stopping caring for him.*
11. *Not being able to sort out his primary schooling for him.*
12. *Being negative and not praising him enough.*
13. *My wish that he would get out of my house and go find an apartment.*

Carol, when we discussed the relative influence guilt has over you as opposed to the influence you have over it, the results showed a trend. Six months ago, 30% of your arguments were for self-respect and 70% for self-torture. Recently you were 40% for self-respect and 60% for self-torture, and today you were 45% for self-respect and 55% for self-torture. You say that survival has driven you in this direction. I believe there is much more to it than that, although I, too, have concerns for your survival in such a degrading situation. However, you are not ready to take some decisive action to go on the offensive until your arguments for self-respect exceed your arguing for self-torture. We came up with two ideas that might tip the balance in the favor of your self-respect so that you might challenge self-torture. The first idea was to send copies of this letter to Jan, Donna, Richard, and Kathy,* in order to seek their opinions as to which course you should take: further self-torture or emergent self-respect. As agreed, I have provided you with copies of this letter for that purpose. When all your replies are back ring me for an appointment so we can assess your readiness. However, I am firmly convinced that your readiness will immediately become apparent to you when you are ready. If your children's responses are unable to convince you to argue more strongly for self-respect, then we will pursue policy 2 as per our discussion. You know as well as I do that it cannot help but do the trick.

Good luck on your preparation for self-affirmation by taking some affirmative actions on your own behalf. Remember, a guilt-driven life is a life sentence.

Best wishes!
D. E.

Three weeks later, Carol rang with great urgency and requested an immediate appointment. She said she just had to tell me something. We met the next day. The following is the text of that meeting, which was immediately typed and forwarded to her:

You said I would know when I was ready. I started to feel resentful. I had two bad days at work. I went home to find a bank account which showed that money had been taken out of my cash point account—$130. He knew my number. I had given him the card at times. He had previously asked me for a loan of $75. The first time was $80, then $10, then $20, then the next day $10. $130 went in three days. I rang the bank and said I wanted to stop the account. I had had a lot of pressure at work. I felt too awful to go to my night class. I drove home. . . . Tony was looking pleased with himself, beer cans everywhere. I didn't know what happened but it felt like

*Carol's four elder children.

something had snapped. I felt I was outside my body. I was scream-
ing and crying at the same time: "I've given, given, given and I've
got no more to give." I saw a big deep hole: "Get out or I'll call the
police." All my fear went . . . everything went out of me. I even had
him physically up against the wall. He went on in his usual way. He
tried all his ways: "Do you want a hug?" He then threatened to
smash my car, break my windows, kill me. I felt terrific—I'm not
afraid anymore. "You can do nothing to me." I was surprised it was
happening. There was this big empty hole with nothing in it. I was
unafraid even though he threatened to hire my killer. I went to my
neighbor who gave me some wine and a tranquillizer. I fell asleep
immediately.

The next day I went to a friend's after work. I rang home and
asked if Diane's* parents were still coming. "Yes," so I returned
home. He introduced us. I didn't offer them coffee or tea. I sat
there in deadly silence. Finally the father said: "Are you and Tony
incompatible?" We both said: "Yes!" I said, "I have had enough!"
The father said, "Have you got any other children?" "Yes, four."
"Can he go anywhere else?" "Yes, his father's." Tony said, "But he
lives in Merivale." I sat there in total silence. Finally he said that
they couldn't have a stranger in their house. I didn't care what they
thought of me . . . this is my home. I want people I want in my
home. I don't want anyone pushing me around anymore. They
went. Then we had an argument about the heater. He smashed it.
He rang his father and asked him if he could stay there. I told him,
"Dad will have to come and get your belongings by Saturday. Sat-
urday is my deadline . . . after that, I will sell your things or give
them away." All he said was "Ah shit!" Tony said to his father, "You
can see how unreasonable she has been." Then he stamped on my
foot but didn't break any bones. He smashed the clock on the way
out. He's gone. He rang me a couple of days later and asked me for
some money. I went and gave him the money and he twisted my
fingers. I felt a twinge of fear. Richard came over and changed the
locks.

Just before I went home that day I was able to tell people at

*Diane was Tony's girlfriend.

work what was happening. Why should I go on pretending any longer? I told a couple of friends. They looked shocked. They told me to change my locks. I think that is coming through to me as important . . . telling other people.

You ask what are the steps that happened after I left you. Well, he wasn't doing anything he hadn't done before. I felt resentful. Why should I put up with this anymore? I sent the letters. I got Donna's back. Jan is half through hers. The reply came after I snapped. Still I suppose they helped. I may need them to refer back to. I didn't know I was as ready as I was. I didn't know I was so close. The first change was telling people what was happening a bit. I couldn't before. I didn't want anyone to think Tony wasn't a nice boy. I looked at an old photograph of Tony when he was 13 — there wasn't anything left of the boy I loved. I didn't want to have anything to do with him if he can't care about people. That's the truth!

It went snap . . . it was really dramatic. I saw myself as a great big hole — that round . . . that dark . . . totally empty . . . nothing even at the bottom. I've given . . . given . . . given . . . it's all gone.

That day, I thought, too, of all the people who have abused me, taken advantage of me when I was trying to be kind to them. I feel like I've been a victim of a lot of people for a long time.

It was the straw that broke the camel's back. It was the money and what had been happening at work. I had struck a few sexist people calling me "Darling." And having to walk all the way to the bank at lunch time. And not being able to go to my lecture after work.

I was very embarrassed about the letters. But each child was very nice. I rang them up beforehand and told them I feel guilty about a lot of things. They were just. They were curious. But it helped. I knew I would get their replies. I think I'll need the letters to refer to. Kicking him out — that was the solution in the back of my mind. It happened just like you said it would. It's wonderful . . . I don't have any more links (money) with his father. A whole new life can start for me. There was no room for compromise once I started. I have been blackmailed by love. Girls are brought up on fairytales of love and romance. I have raised my girls differently.

I didn't tell any of my children. I didn't feel the need. I just felt the need to come back here and tell you.

Carol wrote two weeks later informing me that all was going well. She felt she "couldn't stop loving and caring for Tony" but that she would now insist "he change inside himself":

> *I used to feel a total failure as far as he was concerned but I did my best and I think the rest was up to him. The most I feel now is sad for what happened. . . . It is interesting to think about the process that changed things for me. First I believed in you and trusted you totally—there was no alternative anyway. I did try to think about things as instructed. Sometimes it took as much energy as physical labor would. The steps that stand out are finding I could tell people some of what was happening and feeling surprised that they did not condemn me or say nasty things about Tony to me. Next I felt more and more resentful and that I did not deserve all this. Then you know the rest of what happened. I hope one day the "hole" will fill up again and I will be able to give, but I know I won't ever lose my self-respect again.*
>
> > *Thanks,*
> > *Carol*
>
> *P.S. I passed my exam with 85% and have enrolled in a more advanced course!*

I replied:

Dear Carol,

Many thanks for your letter. You sound like a person freed from a prison, where guilt had been your gaoler. I believe that the emptiness you are now feeling will be filled up by you and your friends sooner than you would think. You are now ready for both personal accomplishments and pleasures. You have had to set yourself aside for so long. Tomorrow belongs to you and I believe that you are more than entitled to it. I agree with you when you say: "I will

never lose my self-respect again." Also, you will never torture yourself again either.
Congratulations on your exam results and good luck on your
new career in life.

Yours respectfully,
D. E.

I wrote Carol a year later asking her permission to publish her
story:

Of course you can use my "story." If it can benefit anyone I will
be more than happy.
Tony and I are getting on better than we have for years. Since
leaving he has gone through various stages from hating me to
asking if he can come and stay at odd times. He is not allowed
drugs or alcohol or his music on loudly all the time but accepts
this.
He was drinking excessively and taking drugs. Now he has decided to stop unless it is offered free and is saving his money, wants
to go back to school as an adult next year and later university.
I am still changing too. I feel a lot more confident and, although
I do not like Tony's tattoos and some of his attitudes, I am proud he
is my son and do like some things about him very much and can
accept him as he is whether he changes further or not.

Regards and best wishes with the book,
Carol

*Remembering to Forget**

Janet, aged 14 years, was referred with her mother to the Leslie
Centre after a suicide attempt which resulted in her hospitaliza-

---

*Co-authored by David Epston and Johnella Bird, Leslie Centre, Auck-
land.

tion. Frances, Janet's mother, was desperate for assistance, as Janet continued to run away from home after her discharge.

Frances and Janet had been living in Auckland for six months. Frances had separated from Janet's father 10 years ago, and Janet's sister, Anne, aged 12, was presently living with him. Frances planned to return to Christchurch (a city approximately 1200kms to the south) in the new year. Both Frances and Janet stated that something changed in Janet's behavior two months ago. She had been overeating, was constantly tired, consequently finding it difficult to wake in the mornings, and had lost all interest in school work, even though she had previously been an accomplished student.

As the interview progressed, it became clear that both Frances and Janet had fled Christchurch as they had been unable to face the consequences of Janet's grandmother's seemingly inexplicable behavior. The story that they told amazed us, and at the end of the session we summarized it and then said that it was critical for both of them, and in particular Janet, to finish this chapter in their lives. We felt that they had contributed to the completion of this chapter by again relating to themselves, and to two strangers, the previously unspeakable facts. We suggested that the more explicit the past became, the less impact it would have on their lives and the readier they would be to begin a new chapter.

The following is a summary of their story:

Janet, you grew up knowing that you had grandparents who cared very much for you. Your grandmother had had an unfortunate, mixed-up life. She grew up missing her father (who had not been involved in her life) and at a young age was sexually molested by her mother's boyfriend. Her mother didn't believe her and consequently treated her very badly. This led her to have serious problems in life. She married and had a daughter. Her daughter had a daughter of her own called Janet. Janet's father disappeared, which resulted in her grandparents' working very hard to substitute for her runaway father—they almost became the "other parent" figure in her life.

It's not surprising that the granddaughter and grandparents were close, and it's possible that the grandmother worked overtime to be close to Janet because of her failure to be close to her own daughter, Frances. Inevitably, Janet, your mother must have got the idea that your grandmother was in competition for you and you became involved in a tug-of-love. Frances believes that you are more loyal to your grandmother than you are to her and that couldn't have helped but upset her.

Then one day you started to receive obscene phone calls that "freaked you out" and these only happened when your mother was out creating a better future for herself by attending the university. Not surprisingly, you would ring your grandmother when you were "freaked out" and she would come around. When Frances came home, your grandmother would look at her like "death warmed up." The phone calls went on and on, and you got more and more "freaked out," and probably found it hard to concentrate on very much. However, in Sherlock Holmes fashion, it turned out that the butler, or the least expected person, was guilty—in this case your grandmother. This must have confused you and must have kept you awake at night wondering—why would your grandmother, who loved you so much, "freak you out"?

The only course of action you could take was to pretend to forget about it and more or less think that nothing had happened. The trouble is that it did happen and in your "subconscious" you are really amazed.

As you write your version of this story, we believe the pieces will fit together in a way tha permits you to remember it so you can really forget it. We know it's impossible to really forget things unless they make sense. This will come to make sense as you write this out of your life.

Don't expect, however, that this will right your mother's disillusionment with your grandmother. That would be too much to ask of you.

We made another appointment in a month's time. However, in the third week I (J. B.) was contacted by Frances, who said that Janet's mood had lifted. She had returned to school and the two of them had begun to talk. Frances added that after the session she had thought about what we had said and had decided to return to Christchurch, because that was where she wanted to be. They were leaving that week. Janet had asked her mother to ring so that she could say goodbye. Janet told me that she felt that she had closed that chapter in her life. She knew that she would be facing difficulties on her return to Christchurch, but felt confident that she could overcome them.

This session illustrates a common occurrence in therapy, that is, the influence of "forgetting" traumatic events. Within the process of this therapy, we provided a safe place for "remembering" and built a context within which Janet and Frances' story could be written and rewritten, thereby allowing them to make a distinction between the past, the present, and the future.

Escape from Retirement

I (M. W.) well remember my first meeting with Harry Saunders. I found him wandering through the passage at Dulwich Centre, looking lost and distressed. Upon introducing myself, I learned that a friend had suggested that he consult me over his son, Paul, who was 16 years old. Harry was very concerned about Paul and felt that the situation was quite desperate.

Approximately two years ago, said Harry, Paul had begun to withdraw and lose confidence. Over a period of months there was an acceleration of this withdrawal, which included school refusal. Various authorities, including those from the school system, attempted to intervene. All of these attempts, including the vigorous and exhaustive efforts to return him to school, failed to have the desired effect. In response, Paul became more introspective and self-critical.

On a couple of occasions, Harry, and Paul's mother, Rose, managed to get him to a clinic. On these occasions he was assessed, diagnosed, and prescribed medication. Each time Paul refused to return for further visits and would not take the medication.

He had withdrawn to the point that he seldom emerged from his bedroom, would speak only to his parents and his younger brother, and even then only rarely. Most of the time he would lie on or behind his bed, at times crying and at times "just throwing things up and down." He had always been a "shy and sensitive" person, but had graduated to become a highly successful recluse.

In response to my question about the effects of this on other family members, Harry said that he and Rose felt almost constantly stressed and distressed, and that their sense of despair was becoming more intense with the passage of time. Paul's younger brother was apparently less affected, but he was also a sensitive person and couldn't, at times, help being preoccupied about the state of his brother's life. He found the fact that he couldn't find any way of helping Paul very difficult to accept.

I arranged a time to meet with the whole family. Harry wasn't at all sure that he could succeed at getting Paul to attend the appointment, and even if he did succeed on the first occasion, was doubtful that he would be able to get him to attend for another. In response, I told Harry that it was not necessary for Paul to attend at all but that it might be helpful even if he came to one meeting.

To Harry's credit, he did manage to get Paul to attend the first appointment with the rest of the family. At the outset of this meeting, everyone was clearly apprehensive, including me. Paul would not maintain eye contact and said very little. He appeared agitated and was certainly unhappy about having to attend the meeting.

Retirement, as a candidate description of an external problem, emerged somewhere early in the session. I do not recall who gave this description, but suddenly there it was, and we were talking about the effects that this was having in the lives and relationships of family members. After investigating its effects, there was a consensus that Paul's retirement in life had been very influential.

When mapping the influence of family members in the life of the problem, we identified several areas in which Paul could have submitted to retirement but hadn't. He had not totally succumbed and wasn't entirely a passenger in life. I invited them all to perform meaning around these unique outcomes, and although Paul's participation in this discussion was far from active, he did seem engaged and somewhat surprised at the turn of events. We also identified occasions when the effects of retirement could have pressed Harry and Rose to suspend activities in their relationship, but when, instead, they resisted. In addition, we discovered that there were various occasions during which retirement could have made them all far more despairing than they were.

Towards the end of our meeting, Paul did give some minimal

indication that both retirement and escape from it had their attractions. Rose, Harry, and James, the younger brother, however, were clear about the possibilities they preferred, and we discussed some of the steps that might be available to them to extend their defiance of the problem's requirements of them and of their relationships.

Paul was noncommittal about the idea of returning for a second session, and I did not see him again. All future communication with him was via his parents, his brother, or through letters.

The first letter of the following series* was sent after the second meeting. I will not discuss these letters in detail, except to say that they reflect some efforts to establish a new receiving context for Paul's experience of his life and for his parents' experience of him. The "old" story that provided the receiving context for experience was, in general terms, one that emphasized failure. The new receiving context is one that makes the attribution of failure very difficult. The therapist's posture of supporting persons from behind rather than from ahead is a primary mechanism for the construction of this new receiving context. As a general rule, persons cannot see unique possibilities for their lives if others are standing in front of them, blocking their view.

For persons who experience themselves as spectacular failures, just to point out positives and to be generally and directly enthusiastic about events in their lives constitute a "disempowering" distinction. Under these circumstances, the person will identify a major discrepancy between where he perceives himself to be in life, on the one hand, and where he believes others perceive him to be, on the other. He will "find" the picture that others have of his life to be way ahead of what he believes to be his actual circumstances, will experience himself as falling short, and will have his sense of failure confirmed. And this confirmation will have very real effects.

Supporting persons from behind is not problematic in this way. The therapist can achieve this position in a general sense by work-

---

*The series that appears here represents only a sample of the letters sent to Peter and his parents.

ing to identify unique outcomes and by directly engaging the person in the performance of new meanings around these. Thus, the person is encouraged to be the privileged author of the new story.

The therapist can also achieve this standing-behind posture by taking up a position at the "base line," against which all of the changes in the person's life can be thrown into sharp relief. This provides for a more empowering distinction. The therapist consistently endeavors to identify with the position at which the person was previously and maintains a cautious attitude, so as not to catch up too quickly with developments in the person's life. This enables the therapist to be "caught off-guard" by these developments and counters the possibility of getting ahead of the person and thus contributing to a disempowering distinction. The therapist can persistently encourage the person to catch her/him up on developments and to provide an understanding of these. As the person experiences himself/herself as more successful, the therapist can afford to be less concerned about the likelihood of getting ahead of him/her.

"Readiness questioning" and speculation can also facilitate both the standing-behind posture for the therapist and the installation of a receiving context that makes the attribution of failure difficult. The therapist can be curious as to how persons knew that they were ready to take the steps that they took, and can inquire into persons' readiness to take any further steps that might be proposed. Thus, whether or not persons take another step in their escape from the influence of the problem is a matter of readiness, not failure. And if persons step back, then an incorrect assessment of readiness to take this step in the first place is the culprit.

Dear Paul,

I am sorry that you didn't come to the appointment on August 11th. I had been looking forward to seeing you again and I missed you. I did, however, respect your decision not to come on this particular occasion. My guess is that you were not ready to come to the meeting and therefore it was probably wise of you not to come. It also gave me a good chance to talk things over with your Mum and Dad.

I learned from them that you have been consolidating some of the steps that you have taken in giving retirement the slip and to pull your own strings. We discussed how it is important that you don't escape too quickly the habits that retirement has coached in your life. It's very important for you to know that progress goes in stops and starts, and often seems like three steps forward and two back.

My speculation is that you have been getting ready to take another step in your escape from retirement. I don't know what this step will be, nor do I know when you will be ready to take it, but would like to urge you not to be too ambitious about it.

I do appreciate what you are doing and really look forward to seeing you again at the next meeting.

Yours sincerely,
M. W.

Dear Paul,

I missed you at the meeting today, Tuesday, September 1st. By telling you this, I'm not trying to put pressure on you to come to the next meeting, but I'm just letting you know that I remain interested in you as a person.

Your Mum and Dad told me that you have had your braces taken off and I'm really looking forward to meeting you again some time so that I can see the difference that this makes to you. I bet you are delighted.

You may remember that in the last letter I said that I thought that all evidence proved that you were getting ready to take another step in your escape from retirement. Although I thought this was the case, I wasn't exactly sure. I was looking forward with great anticipation to hearing about the news and was delighted to hear that you took that step on Saturday, August 22nd. Mind you, I hadn't expected such a big step, so the news did catch me a little off-guard. On that day you acted on your own behalf and made a contribution in a way you haven't in well over a year.

To you, this must have been an important signpost to your future as a person who can direct his own life and who is able to appreciate those things that are special to him.

In view of the fact that you were ready to go a bit further than I had thought you were, my guess is that your next step is not too far up the road. I am trying to imagine what this step might be.

I look forward to the next installment.

Yours sincerely,
M. W.

P.S.: I am sure that you know not to go too fast.

Dear Paul,

I meant to send this letter off to you a couple of weeks ago but got caught up with a conference.

I recently met with your parents again and learned of the new steps you have been taking in your escape from retirement.

I must say that I was surprised by some of these new steps and initially didn't know quite what to say. I must admit that I was virtually struck speechless when I was informed that you had followed through with the play and that your competence was suddenly available for everyone to see. This was an achievement that I hadn't thought you were ready for and your success has certainly had a big effect on my picture of you as a person. Don't get me wrong, I've always known that you had the capacity to direct your own life but, as I previously mentioned, you were already well ahead of schedule in your comeback.

Your parents told me about a lot of other things that they had noticed about your emerging competence and confidence and I won't comment on all of these, except to say that they firmly establish the fact that you have consolidated your new course in life. All those who care to see could not be blind to the depth of this new direction.

Despite this, I was a little perturbed when your parents reported your decision to go to school this year. Initially I wanted to tell your parents that it was too soon for you to take this step and that they should discourage you from proceeding with it. We then discussed the matter further and we could not work out whether you were yet ready to take such a step. I said that my apprehension and insecurity about this might be lessened if you would agree to consider going to school as an experiment to see if you were really ready for this step. If you are saying, "I am going to school this year and will see it through," then this makes me very jumpy and extremely nervous. If, however, you are saying, "I am going to experiment with going to school this year to see if I am ready for it," then I would feel just a bit more relaxed.

I have enormous respect for you over the steps that you have already taken and I have told some of my colleagues about you (without mentioning your name). Word is getting around that in the past eight months you have set a cracking pace in your escape from the clutches of retirement in life, and most believe that it would be quite acceptable for you to now sit back and have a rest from your progress.

If you ever do reach a point where you decide to come in and meet with me, I would be delighted to see you again. You see, my picture of you as a person has so much changed that I am extremely curious about how you now look.

All the best for '88.

Warm regards
M. W.

Dear Paul,

I recently met with your parents again. They filled me in on recent developments in your life.

I personally found the meeting with them quite helpful. The information they gave was good for me to have because, as you may recall, our last meeting left me feeling a bit nervous about the speed of your progress. I had been worried that you might have been getting too far ahead of schedule. You had been taking further steps to dismiss retirement from your life. In fact, on a couple of occasions you had entirely walked out on retirement. Perhaps I was jolted by this news because at some level I may have believed that you were only having a vacation from retirement.

I previously had only a sketchy account of this new picture of you as a person. Only recently have I been able to grasp, more fully, the significance of the steps that you are taking. This has helped me realize that these steps are for real.

It's now sinking in that, all along, you have been determined to break out of the corner that retirement had pushed you into. Thanks to your recent achievements I feel that I have been able to join you on firmer ground. I hope that you will understand that my insecurity related to the fact that I had got left behind to some extent.

I talked about the situation to some of my colleagues (without mentioning your name, of course) and they wanted to know more about you. They were very curious about your life, asking many questions about how you had achieved as much as you have in the past months. They tried to imagine what words of advice you have been giving to yourself, and how you had thrown a spanner in the works of retirement and outstripped all predictions. I'm sorry that I wasn't able to fully satisfy their curiosity. If we do get to meet at some point in the future, you might be interested to hear some of these questions.

One colleague thought that perhaps I was getting too far ahead of myself, that I should restrain my enthusiasm for what you are doing, and caution you to slow down. I said that the information your parents had given suggested that the rate of your progress was suiting you and that he should calm down. What do you think?

I look forward with anticipation to hearing further news.

Regards,
M. W.

Dear Rose and Harry,

I enjoyed catching up with you again on Paul's progress. I was writing to Paul and decided to send you a letter as well.

I found the details you gave about Paul's rediscovery of himself and of life very refreshing. I do understand that it is a profound experience for you to see your son losing his future and nearly losing himself and then to see him embracing a new life and a new future. As you have said, it's difficult to find the right words to adequately describe such an experience.

Of course, in your appreciation of what Paul has been achieving, it would be all too easy for you to underestimate your own contributions to his re-emergence in life. I would be opposed to this, as I believe that the steps a person takes should always be visible to that person.

It hasn't all been clear sailing. At times you have thought that Paul was wavering, appearing to take a step back. At these times you didn't allow your new picture of him to become overshadowed and you refused to join him in despair. This helped him turn his back on despair.

You have had to do what is very difficult for parents to do in the circumstances in which you found yourselves. As Paul began to pioneer a new direction in life, you had to restrain your enthusiasm and encouragement so as not to get ahead of him. Even on those occasions when you momentarily succumbed, you quickly realized and took immediate steps to get behind him instead. And at these times you worked at avoiding self-criticism.

Recently, with your permission, I showed a brief excerpt of a videotape of one of our meetings at a seminar that was attended by a large number of counselors. This raised a lot of interest. They heard you vividly describing your experience and appreciated your willingness to share this with them.

There were many enthusiastic comments and many questions, far too numerous for me to record. This included questions about how you had known what were the more helpful ideas in your mission to assist Paul, how you resisted pressure from relatives and friends to abandon your new approach and instead do what they believed was natural, and what you had learned about how to assist young people like Paul that could be passed on to other parents facing the sort of circumstances that you have faced.

These are not questions that you should feel compelled to answer, but you might like to think them over.

I look forward to our next meeting.

Regards,
M. W.

The developments in Paul's life were not the only foci of attention during our meetings. Rose and Harry identified other aspects of the problem's requirements in their lives, and took many steps to extend their protest against these. As they perceived these steps to be undermining of the problem, they developed a new account of themselves as parents and became more hopeful about Paul's escaping from retirement. There did come a time when they had to do what seemed very unnatural to them; they had to struggle to contain their hope so as not to get ahead of Paul. However, they did succeed in taking up a position behind him and engaged him in a readiness inquiry.

Over a period of 10 months, Paul inched himself out of retirement, began to experiment with going to school again, developed a close friendship with a peer, became engaged in a social network, and found himself facing a new future. Other family members became less apprehensive about him and were able to attend to aspects of their lives that had been put on hold for some time.

Recruiting a Wider Audience

At times I (M. W.) send letters with the purpose of summarizing the new developments that are visible in persons' lives, as well as the understandings arrived at in relation to these new developments. This seems strongly indicated when the new meanings that have been generated around unique outcomes seem particularly tenuous, when there is a considerable risk that the new story will enter the shadow of the old and thus become imperceptible to persons.

The following provides an example of such correspondence and relates to meetings with Marlene and Dick. Marlene was 27 years of age when she was referred to the family therapy unit of a large state psychiatric hospital. At this time she had a nine-year history of depression, anxiety, anorexia nervosa, bulimia, and other forms of self-abuse. She had been the recipient of numerous treatments over this time, including those that had required hospitalizations. These hospitalizations had included detainment.

At our first meeting with Marlene, she was so frail and emaciated that we were surprised that she was surviving. She was over five feet and ten inches tall, and her weight ws somewhat below 40 kilograms (88 pounds). She would not sit down, but stood hunched in the corner of the interviewing room. There she remained physically active throughout our meeting, alternating between wringing her hands and wrapping and unwrapping her arms around her body. She was clearly very anxious about the meeting and did not speak. Her dyspepsia was very audible. We did not understand how Dick had managed to succeed in getting her to come to the interview.

With what appeared to be Marlene's blessing, Dick provided some background detail. Marlene had ben subjected to a great deal of emotional and physical abuse as a child and adolescent, mostly perpetrated by her father, but also by a neighbor and one of her grandmothers. This had included violent sexual assault. For some part of this, her mother had held her responsible. She was constantly told that she was nothing but rubbish, and her father justified his actions by informing her that he had taken it upon himself to beat the badness out of her.

Marlene had become anorectic at the age of 17. She had married Dick when she was 24. She had met him through correspondence (as a pen pal). Dick had been very concerned for her and had believed that he would be able to help her put her life together. However, despite his best efforts, he found Marlene's anorexia nervosa, depression, and anxiety to be relentless.

We met together for a few sessions. Marlene's self-hate coaches were identified, self-hate was externalized, and the effects of this were mapped. Several unique outcomes, for both Marlene and Dick, were located. In these meetings, Marlene remained standing. However, by the end of the second session she was participating by whispering some comments to Dick, which he then relayed on to me.

It was established that these unique outcomes meant that Marlene was beginning to separate from her father's attitude towards her. In turn, this suggested that the future of self-hate had become a little insecure. Letters were sent that summarized the developments that had been observed and that encouraged further performances of meaning around unique outcomes.

Suddenly, Dick called to cancel the next appointment, saying that Marlene didn't want to attend any more meetings. She had decided that we were wasting our time. I protested that we did not believe that this was the case, but Marlene could not be persuaded of this.

I called for a two-year follow-up. I spoke to Dick. Marlene was still alive, although not in very good shape. She would not speak on the phone, so I had to be content to have Dick pass on my regards to her. The next day, Dick called and said that Marlene had expressed a desire to return for some more meetings. I was delighted and arranged to see them immediately.

Although Marlene still looked very frail, she did manage to sit down for part of the meeting. I asked what had discouraged Marlene from persisting with our initial meetings and what had prompted her to reinstitute them now.

Her response to this, as relayed by Dick, was that she hadn't thought that she "had deserved it." I was immediately concerned about what I said that could have upset her so, and asked that she tell me about this. However, I had misunderstood her comment. What she meant was that, since she believed that she was "rub-bish," she did not think that she was worthy of all the attention that she was receiving from us.

The fact that Marlene had felt entitled to request further appointments, coupled with the fact that she had allowed herself to sit down, was indeed indicative of some important developments. Upon encouraging Dick and Marlene to help me understand this, I discovered that Marlene had taken further steps at separating from her father's attitude towards her, and had been developing a new and more accepting relationship with herself. That she was sitting down clearly illustrated this. She was no longer subscribing to her father's idea that she "didn't deserve to sit on chairs because she would inevitably soil them."

Several months have now passed since the first of our second series of meetings; the following letters to Marlene and Dick provide an account of these meetings.

Dear Marlene,

I have enjoyed my recent meetings with you. I fact, I have found it quite refreshing to witness the steps that you have been taking against self-hate and against anorexia nervosa. This letter summarizes some of our reflections, and includes some questions that will help us deal with our curiosity.

Our attention was very much drawn to the evidence that you were becoming more interested in your own life. You had become concerned about yourself and, for the first time, believed that you had a right to have your own life and future.

This told us that you had weakened self-hate. Later we discovered that you had been hitting yourself less, that you had been less rejecting of yourself. This told us that you now have the ability to take your own side.

The news that you had realized that you were separating from your father's and grandmother's attitude towards yourself was spectacular news. After all the training you received in being everyone else's person, after all the coaching you had in rejecting yourself, this rejection of your father's and your grandmother's attitude towards yourself is really something else.

- *How did you achieve this step in separation without being crushed by guilt, without apologizing for yourself, without torturing yourself?*
- *How has this step in the reclaiming of yourself changed your attitude to your body?*
- *Do you think this has undermined the claims on your body that others have made in the past?*

Please do not feel any obligation to answer these questions. However, if you have any thoughts about them, and if you feel all right about sharing such thoughts with us, this would help us with our understanding.

In weakening self-hate, we could see that you had already begun a new history that is entirely different from your old history, a new history that is attached to a new future.

We look forward to seeing you again and catching up on developments.

Kind regards,
M. W.

Dear Marlene and Dick,

We really enjoyed catching up with you on Thursday, December 22nd, and thought that you might like a brief summary of the meeting.

Marlene, it was clear to all of us that you had progressed a very long way since the previous meeting, even though you had not fully realized the extent of this. You had taken some very great steps in your escape from all of the early training that you were given in being a person for your father and your mother. Instead, you had been investigating new ways of being your own person.

You have been protesting against keeping your feelings hidden and protesting against everyone else having your mind for you. Instead you have been discovering ways to express many of these previously hidden feelings and you have been finding your own voice in which to express your own opinions. And you drew our attention, at the end of the session, to the importance of your own signature. This confirmed our view about the extent to which you have been making progress. We are looking forward in anticipation to news of further developments.

Dick, we were impressed by some of the realizations that you have been having about the danger of accepting invitations to have a mind for Marlene, and also impressed with the speed at which you were able to identify possibilities for declining such invitations in the future. It is clear that, in so doing, you are supporting Marlene in her project of becoming her own person. We could also see that you were able to look beyond the immediate discomfort that you have experienced in relation to Marlene's expression of her feelings and opinions, and that you see this as a very important breakthrough in her life and in your relationship with her.

Just as it can be seen that there is new growth in Marlene's garden, so it can also be seen that there is new growth in your lives and in your relationship.

I look forward to our next meeting with you.

Regards,
M. W.

Dear Marlene and Dick,

We really enjoyed meeting with you again last Thursday. This letter is a summary of our two recent meetings. I will refer to them separately.

1. Second Last Meeting

During the meeting we discovered that there had been some very significant developments in the lives of Marlene and Dick, and in their relationship as well.

Marlene had found herself with a stronger voice in this relationship. She had been expressing her feelings and opinions to him more effectively and directly, and had realized that she was pleased with this development. In so doing, Marlene had commenced the work of identifying herself, of working out what suits her and what doesn't, of what appeals to her and what doesn't.

This told us all that Marlene was more trusting of herself and more appreciative of her own thoughts. And the fact that she had found renewed interest in food and the garden told us all that her life was coming alive. Marlene had also been "feeling the woman coming out" in her, and was pleased about this, but also scared that this could lead to sexual expectations from Dick.

For Dick's part, he found that he had been confronting the habit of having Marlene's mind for her. In fact, he had reduced the habit's influence in his life by 25%. He had also weakened the habit of not fully appreciating Marlene's experience, and instead had further developed his listening skills.

In escaping the domination of old habits and in contributing to new possibilities for the relationship, Dick had experienced a flexibility in himself that no-one, including himself, could have predicted. Thus it was clear that Dick had an increased capacity to intervene in his life.

With regard to the relationship between Marlene and Dick, it was no longer overtaken by despair. In taking their relationship away from despair, they were witnessing the emergence of new developments in their communication and in their problem-solving ability.

At the end of this meeting, both Dick and Marlene agreed that it would be unwise to rush things at this stage by getting too intimate with each other, and agreed that they should absolutely abstain from any sexual relationship until they both felt entirely ready to do so.

2. Last Meeting

The facts that Marlene and Dick gave at the last meeting surprised us all. Although we had predicted that they would take some new steps, what they had achieved in the weeks between this meeting and the last went way past our expectations, and we needed to take out considerable time to catch up with them.

Although they had been more openly discussing their differences, they had not had one serious quarrel. In trying to understand this, we all thought that this reflected a further development in their relationship's problem-solving ability. It was also noted that the relationship was more balanced, in that now Marlene was experiencing herself being helpful to Dick and Dick was now opening himself up to Marlene's support. This was particularly apparent in the discussions that they had been having about the pressures that Dick is currently facing in his workplace.

Marlene had taken further steps in siding with being her own person. She had proceeded to do this despite the fact that her mother had been uncomfortable about it. These steps were providing us, and others, with news about how Marlene is developing an accepting relationship with herself and separating from a rejecting relationship with herself—news about how she is becoming a self-embracing person rather than self-erasing person. These steps also reflect the extent to which Marlene now feels that she has the right to be happy.

We recognized that Dick had extended his listening skills into other areas of the relationship, and that he was also finding that it was becoming easier for him to reflect on both his own and Marlene's experience. He had also proceeded to further undermine the habit that had been encouraging him to have a mind for Marlene. Dick was well aware of the benefits of the work that he was doing as he said that he thought that they were "now getting over the rough period."

I hope that this summary is a reasonably accurate one of our last two meetings. We look forward in anticipation to meeting with you again so that we might catch up on further developments in your lives and relationships, developments that could be based on the recent discoveries that you have been making about yourselves.

Regards,
M. W.

Marlene treasures these letters and reads them through many times. She has responded to most of them with letters of her own. In these letters she gives testimony to her experiences of abuse as a child and adolescent.

Although Marlene still feels that her father has some hold on her life, she is pleased that she has been able to weaken this. And recently, for the first time, she has refused her mother's demands on her and has not been overwhelmed by guilt in the process. No longer does she constantly refer to herself as rubbish, and she has stopped beating herself with her fists. She is taking in a little more protein and speaks more strongly and directly with her own voice.

Dick and Marlene have made considerable headway in their relationship. They are talking their conflicts out more fully and listening more closely to each other's experience.

The work that we are doing together is ongoing. I suggested to Marlene and Dick that I include a brief description of their experience here, as well as some of the letters that summarize discussions that we have had. They thought that this could be a good idea, particularly as they have felt so alone in their struggle to free their lives and their relationship from the influence of self-hate. Publishing this description in this way is another step towards undermining the isolation to which this self-hate had confined them. In addition, they understand that, in making these details available, they may assist others to realize that they are not alone in their struggle to reclaim their lives.

So, you, the reader, are being recruited as an audience to Dick and Marlene's performance of new meanings and expression of a new story. In this way you are contributing to the survival of this new story. And, if Marlene and Dick are curious enough about your experience of this performance, then you are also contributing to the elaboration of this new story. You might even be prepared to write to them about your response to this information about their struggle.* They would be very interested to have any

---

*Send all responses to Marlene and Dick, c/o Michael White, Dulwich Centre, 345 Carrington Street, Adelaide, South Australia, 5000, Australia.

such responses, as long as they are not expected to reply. They are quite clear about the current need to channel all of their available energy to the more immediate and pressing tasks at hand.

SELF STORIES

I (D. E.) often invite people to record their own stories. Customarily, the avowed purpose is to render their story in a form that might be available to others. I have employed a wide range of media: videotape, audiotape, testimonial letters, stories in various genres, personal letters, and the telephone. The narrative structure of these recordings is conventionally that of a "success" story rather than the "sad tale" format of many psychotherapy narratives.

> If a person can manage to present a view of his current situation which shows the operation of favorable personal qualities, it may be called a success story. If the facts of a person's past and present are extremely dismal, then about the best he can do is to show that he is not responsible for what has become of him, and the term sad tale is appropriate. (Goffman, 1961, p. 139)

Writing "success" stories transforms the relationship of the person or family to the problem, as well as the person/family's relationship to the therapy. It has the effect of distancing persons from the problem, and it enables them to "consult" to others as well as themselves should the problem re-emerge in their lives. The discovery of the value of these recorded stories in assisting persons to consult themselves was serendipitous. I previously published an example of utiilizing recordings in this way with the N. family (Epston & Brock, 1984), which had a child with an intractable feeding problem. The N. family had agreed to allow an audio recording of their discussion of the ways in which they had managed to resolve their problem to be made available to other families experiencing similar problems.*

*For a review of this audiotape, see Meadows, 1985.

After the first session with a new family experiencing similar problems, this audio recording was offered to them. This usually had a substantial impact, as the problem usually resolved itself between sessions.

However, the N. family later recontacted the agency at three crisis points: the announcement of another pregnancy, mother's departure for hospital, and mother's return home. On each occasion the family members were advised to listen yet again to their copy of their recording. There was no other contact apart from these three phone calls, and the problem abated each time.

Reviewing other people's "success stories" or testimonials has also had dramatic results, and I am continually building up a library of such resources in the various media. The following are some examples:

Jerry

Jerry, aged 10, had been stealing for some time, so much so in fact that he had been sent to live with various "aunties." Such arrangements broke down very quickly, as soon as he started robbing them blind. In therapy Jerry regained his honest reputation.

Jerry chose verse instead of prose for his "story."

Freddy the Frog

Freddy the frog was a thief.
He was dishonest too.
His family were troubled
in grief.
And nobody knew what to do.

One day he went to a frog clinic,
with lots of kindness in it.
They helped him how to be
honest and true.
And stop his stealing too.
For honesty is the greatest
thing to do.

For Freddy is trusted and his
family aren't sad for Freddy has
them all glad.

I understand Freddy.
I've been like that too.
All through my life I used
to cause strife.
But I'm better now and I'll do my
best to always stay happy and
be like the rest.

Dane

I (D. E.) met with Dane, aged 9, and his parents ten weeks after the birth of Brady. Dane's tantrums had always been a problem, but now they had become much worse. His behavior had deteriorated badly at school. He was unable to resist any teasing and was responding with brutal attacks and biting. After several meetings, Dane had got a grip on himself, and his parents had instituted "special time" for Dane after his brothers had fallen asleep. However, when both Rogan, aged six, and Brady had to be briefly hospitalized, Dane's temper and moods made a comeback on him. We all discussed this and marveled at how the previous solution had so emotionally strengthened Dane. No-one could see any reason why this couldn't happen again. Dane was requested to write his story:

The Importance of Attention

Once there was a boy called John. John was emotionally very strong because he got lots of attention and because he went lots of places. One day he started getting weaker because his mother had a baby boy called Tim. His mother and father started to pay less attention to him and so his temper made a comeback against him.

He started fighting and hurting people and afterwards he felt sorry that he had done it and yet he did not want to apologize to the person. He also started having more tantrums and not wanting to do things to be helpful and he wanted to be paid for everything.

His mother and father got sick of him wanting to have things done without doing anything for anyone else. By now Tim was nearly two years old and could look after himself so John's mother and father could pay more attention and take him more places. John started to get strong again and he stopped his fighting and hurting people. So his mother and father said, "You can have some people to come for tea," because he had stopped his fighting and meanness.

John felt happy and more grown-up and he knew he could keep strong if someone cared about him.

Undertaking a New Initiative*

Jay, aged 13, was referred by his pediatrician regarding his headaches and abdominal pain. Recently, he had spent three weeks in bed, incapacitated with headaches. To some extent, Jay was intolerant of life, had become "mood controlled," and had tantrums at home and school when he was disturbed or interrupted. He had taken to strategically retreating to bed, where he would dream up creative ideas. And the more he retreated, the more others were invited to advance into his life and take the initiative for him. It was obvious that Jay was an extremely able young man.

The team** read and sent the following message/letter to Jay, his sister Mardie, aged 11, and his parents, Blair and Janis.

Dear Janis, Blair, Jay, and Mardie:

Jay, we were all pretty worried for you. We all have grown up and life isn't easy but we think that your strategic retreating habit is tricking you into a secondhand life, a life initiated for you by your parents. However, no creative person your age would really want to take instructions from his parents, even though yours undoubtedly have lots of very good ideas. We suspect you would rather subscribe to "learning by discovery" but warn you that this is far more

---

*Co-authored by Jay Harkness and David Epston.
**The Advanced Family Therapy Training Team: Sohrab Gandomi, Lesley McKay, Wally McKenzie, Lyndsay Thompson, Trish deVillier, Chris Wareing, Louise Webster.

difficult than "learning by instruction." What we couldn't understand was the way you are cheating yourself out of life by with-
drawing and going backwards. No wonder you are so frustrated
because you must know, at some level, that your life is passing you
by. This is probably why you are so vulnerable to moods and passiv-
ity. Lyndsay thought that your creativity is being too restricted and
also worried that your parents and sister, if they don't keep on the
alert, will fall for the "misery loves company" trap. We would fore-
see a time when all of you may start retreating in the vain hope
that keeping Jay's moodiness company will do the trick. The trick
may instead be at your family's expense. The more the Harkness
family sides, inadvertently, with moodiness and panders to its
whims, the more likely Jay will experience his life as running away
from him instead of him being in charge of it and making his own
discoveries about it.

Everyone was of one mind regarding the question: Is Jay able?
The way, as yet undiscovered, how you, Jay, hit your headaches on
the head is impressive evidence in favor of your ability once it has
a direction. The question which we couldn't answer and found
ourselves in a debate about was: Is Jay ready?

*Louise thought that things would have to get a lot worse before
Jay took it upon himself to direct his life instead of being mis-
directed by moodiness. When I asked her what advice she had to
offer in the meantime, she suggested a Woolrest sleeper. She said
that if Jay was going to sleep his growing up away, he might as well
do it in style and comfort. Everyone else was up in arms with this
suggestion for the following reasons:*

1. *If you, Jay, become a Rip Van Winkle character, will you
   wake up in time before it's too late?*
2. *Lyndsay worried that your creativity would be nipped in
   the bud.*
3. *Your parents' energy will be drained away from their own
   creative pursuits in their attempts to provide you with a
   firsthand life. Janis and Blair, everyone agreed that a firsthand life was preferrable to a secondhand life.*

To prove your readiness, Jay, the Team suggests the following:

> *that between now and when we meet again, if you are
> ready (we, once again, want you to know we have no doubts
> about your ability), you will initiate several approaches to a
> more self-embracing (instead of a self-erasing) lifestyle with-
> out your Mum or Dad providing you with either an initia-
> tive or an instruction. For example, washing the boat with-
> out being asked. Jay, you are to keep a list of each and
> every one of your initiatives and not divulge them to your
> parents. Janis and Blair, you are to keep a secret list noting
> any initiatives you have observed Jay taking.*

*Trish wanted you all to know that she recently read Albert Ein-
stein's autobiography. She said that Albert didn't make excuses
when his parents asked him to do his share of the family work.*

*Jay, you also agreed to start writing a history of how you decided
against a secondhand life of retreatism and opted for a firsthand
life of self-direction and discovery.*

We all look forward to catching up with you again.

Fond regards,
D. E.

We met two months later. The following is the team's summary:

Dear Janis, Blair, Jay, and Mardie:

*The team was as staggered as you were, Blair and Janis. Jay, we
knew you had the ability; we were not sure about your readiness;
And we were certainly unprepared for your speed. It's as if you are
now leading your life like a 100-meter sprinter. Jay, you obviously
went home, thought things over, came to your own conclusions,
and then took off. The team was glad that I tape-recorded the
session as the team members didn't feel they could keep pace with
you and, more particularly, with what you've gone and done. We
are wondering whether we are slowing down with age or you are*

overdoing it. Life is like a marathon — you need to hold some energy back for the rest of the race. You can't run your whole life like a
100-meter sprint. Unless you start pacing yourself, most of the
team was worried that you will buckle under or strain yourself.
This is not to imply that you have not made a remarkable comeback. If you hadn't reversed the direction you were heading, you
could have got into trouble and even led a troubled life. Our advice
is that you consider a more moderate pace, one which means you
will be able to go the distance. Lesley drew our attention to the
fact that she believes that you are already doing this. She said:
"Sure he started off with a hiss and a roar but he is now finding his
own pace, one which is comfortable and sustainable." We thought
about her comments and we finally agreed with her. Lesley also
thinks you will go a little bit faster and then a little slower until you
find just the **right** pace for you. She wouldn't be surprised if you
overtaxed yourself on the odd occasion but she knows you will get
it right.

We also acknowledge that you have become something of an
expert in time management and wonder if this isn't something of a
career direction for you.

The team intends to set aside some study time to go over your
"comeback" diary as soon as you submit it. Some of us have a
personal interest in organizing ourselves better in the morning.
Louise also wanted to tell you that, with people like you around,
she's glad she didn't invest in Woolrest sleepers.

Best wishes,
D. E.

Jay was given a tape of the session to assist him in writing up his
"comeback" diary. I received this four months later:

I have undertaken a new initiative. About halfway through the
second term of this year, I realized that life ws basically slipping
away. I was doing plenty of activities — yachting, horseriding, attending classes for skilled writing as well as gifted children, running in school teams, participating in judo classes, etc., but these
were all initiated by others.

I relied on my parents, for example, for transport assistance, etc., as well as the original initiation. In between these activities was a slump, a space of time, where I would be left to my own devices. I had plenty of good ideas, but an essential ingredient—motivation—there was a distinct lack of motivation.

I was basically a slave to what could be termed as "mood control"! The days were slipping away continuously because of persistent interruptions. For instance, after school I'd come in, watch TV, read something, etc. By the time I got round to doing something, there would be interruption or something—e.g., TV program, etc. This is how I become controlled by my inadequacy to confront these things. I recognized this, and became frustrated. Frustration soon turned to anger, which I in turn took out on others. Because of my anger, and my taking it out on others, I was rejected at school. I would lose my temper at home. Then came: "tactical withdrawal"—spending many hours a day doing basically nothing.

It was all very productive in terms of good ideas, yet these only served to frustrate me as I could not achieve them.

This was not a state familiar to me. Basically I became like this in my second year at intermediate. . . . What caused it, I don't know.

But the cure soon became apparent. Organization. When one examined the core of the problem, one found that I was like a sheep browsing from patch to patch of grass. I realized this fairly early in the year, but did nothing about it until July 21st—the day after an appointment at the Leslie Centre.

I suddenly realized there was no easy method of self-improvement, it had to be done the hard way. I redesigned my entire day from start to finish. Where, say, getting organized for school had taken two hours, I managed to reduce it to only 10 minutes. This was the same for all other daily requirements. I then began to include other activities, e.g., jogging, bike riding, etc. Though it took me some time to achieve this, it worked well. The end result of all this was an improved amount of production time, as well as providing a deterrent to becoming distracted by the simple element of time.

As a direct result of this I became less moody, more generous. As well as not recycling gripes. When occasionally I do get annoyed or provoked by something, I do not withhold it, rather let it out in a way which is both tactful and controlled. As well, I have learned to push myself more, making one final effort to round off a good deed, for instance.

But best of all, I've learned to get on better with people, and become a much happier person.

I realized new methods to old distractions, for instance, if there was a problem, a way of solving it would be to write it down. The problem on one side of the page, solution on the other column. Though I basically realized the solution — writing it down made it seem more feasible, by sort of stepping out from the realm of the problem, to get it into perspective as a foreign individual. It is things like this which helped a great deal.

Organizing my day to the full and taking a philosophical aproach to things enable me to use the hours in the day to the full, enabling me more time for my writing, art, yachting, etc., as well as activities I was unable to do before. I now set myself research assignments, which in turn have aided my school work, reports have suddenly been of even a much higher standard than those previous to my initiative.

I now am proud to say that I enjoy life to the full. I have become a much more strong, defined, successful and motivated individual. But what makes me happiest is, though it sounds like some exorbitant claim by some religion or group, I know that it is all of my own accord.

Jay Harkness

Consulting to Yourself

Tracey-Maree called four years after I (D. E.) had first met her family. She was now 20 years old. She told me that she had been depressed for the last three months and just couldn't get out of it. I found it easy to remember her, as she had been one of my most valued "consultants." Her consultancy took the form of a letter of advice she had entrusted to me to give to others who were trapped in the problem she had escaped from. Her letter read:

Hi,

My name is Tracey-Maree and I had the same problem that you've got but with the help of David I overcame it.

My parents separated quite some time ago and during their marriage my father hit my mother. After a year after the separation, with my father continually calling, I started to have bad dreams or else I could not sleep.

David helped me to close my mind to these thoughts by playing a "happy" video in my mind — rather like a movie projector — when these nasty thoughts came. I made this "film" with the help of David beforehand and could play it on demand.

I found that this worked for a week or two but then I got bored with the "film" so I'd change it.

Sometimes I got these bad thoughts of my father coming when I was alone in the house. (He had done this a few times — by coincidence.) I would mentally and physically fight him — and win. When these got really dramatic, I could not play the "film" as my mind would switch itself back. I wouldn't even be able to read or play a record. I would ring a friend and, if possible, go out.

I never used to talk to my friends about my problems at home unless joking. It is only recently that I have started talking to one friend and it really helps. My relationship was improved as my friend felt trusted and helpful.

I have gone through the stage of fear and hatred for my father now and I haven't seen him for a long time. I think what helped me a lot was the knowledge that it wasn't wrong for me to hate my father; he deserved it. Hate is a human feeling and we have to learn to control it, not letting it take over our lives.

What I think is good though is to go out and have a good time with your friends; don't let this ruin the relationships you have. I hope you have a special friend you can talk to. If not, feel free to ring me and I don't mind listening.

Well, I think that's all I have to say and I hope that you get happy soon.

Lots of luv,
Tracey-Maree

Seeing her again after so many years was a great pleasure. She told me she had become a "bitch" to both her friends and family. She was once again acutely aware of injustice. This related to the abuse of her mother's generosity by her 18-year-old brother, Tim. Tracey-Maree found herself persistently drawing her mother's attention to this abuse, but her mother was constrained from taking any action by what she referred to as "a mother's love." Tracey-Maree would then withdraw into her bedroom feeling anger and hatred towards Tim and would become so preoccupied with this that "my heart feels sore."

Tracey-Maree and her mother were now set on separate courses that pitted her "hatred" against "a mother's love." This led to imbroglios between them, with Tracey-Maree "losing respect for mum, snapping, and walking away" at the same time as "feeling guilty because I love her." She then would "talk about it to myself. . . . I have transferred my hatred from my father to Tim. . . . The guilt says that perhaps I should give Tim another chance . . . but there comes a point when I've had enough—it's like punishing myself. I apologize and walk away from it." I posed this question to her: "Are you putting your mother to the test of choosing between Tim's abuse and your depression?" She nodded, "Yes."

I asked about her friends. She had graduated from high school in the previous year but remained at home to work, while all of her seven best friends had either traveled overseas or left Auckland for further study or work. I arranged to meet Tracey-Maree again in three weeks' time.

I dug up her "consultant's letter" and appended this note.

Dear Tracey,

I thought I would like to return the favor. I don't think I could give you any better advice than your advice. By taking your own advice, you are a self-counselor. And by doing so you add more weight to your own counsel. I wonder if the departure of so many of your friends, in whom you confided, for overseas weakened you and you did not feel confident enough to entrust others with your confidences. Concerns such as yours can make comebacks at your most vulnerable times.

If by any chance your depression hasn't departed, read your letter over and over again. Tracey-Maree knows what she is talking about.

Best wishes for the happiness you deserve.

D. E.

Tracey called to cancel our next appointment. She told me that she had gone home and "discussed everything with Mum" and this seemed to resolve her concerns for her mother and her brother. She reported that she had also started to confide in a new group of friends. And her depression had disappeared.

A Release from the Curse of Perfection*

Carolyn rang me and told me, with some reluctance, of the problem she and Tony were having with their daughter, Marissa, aged 11. For some years, Marissa had been overworking on her homework and this had now reached impossible proportions. Marissa required of herself that she do six hours of homework on week days, and seven hours per day on weekends. Everything she did had to be perfect. Carolyn was required by Marissa to see that perfection was achieved. If Carolyn didn't participate perfectly, Marissa felt entitled to kick or revile her in order to bring her into line. I (D. E.) diagnosed a curse: the "curse of the idea of perfection." I contended that this curse would be a life sentence if it went unchallenged. I stated my own preference: five years in Mt. Eden Gaol. With that, at least you could serve your time and get it over with. There is no release from a life sentence under such a curse.

I met with Carolyn, Tony, and their children; Marissa, Michael, aged nine, and Shane, aged four. Every time that either Carolyn or Tony attempted to describe their concerns to me, Marissa would correct them — that is, until I reproved her for this. I informed her,

---

*Co-authored by Carolyn Storey, Tony Storey, and David Epston.

rather bluntly, that I was interested in her parents' opinions and that when I wanted hers I would direct a question to her. Her participation was very limited from there on. I introduced the idea of a homework lifestyle and the support system required for this and asked questions such as: Who fuels the homework lifestyle? Who provides encouragement/finances/resources for Marissa's homework lifestyle? I asked Carolyn if she'd had a training in servitude. At the time she was unable to answer this question.

At the end of the first meeting, we agreed on the following:

1. Tony is to prepare a statement stating that Carolyn is no longer responsible for her daughter's homework and that she will no longer support Marissa's homework lifestyle. Tony will state that he will take responsibility for Marissa's homework and he will support her homework lifestyle as he sees fit. He is to go with Carolyn to a solicitor's office and have his plan notarized. Tony is to provide Marissa with a copy and explain it to her.

2. Carolyn is to go to the Central Public Library and find a book on American history that has a copy of the *Declaration of Independence* in it. She is to rewrite it to suit her own circumstances.

3. Tony and Carolyn are to hold *secret* escape meetings every night in order to discuss ways of escaping the problem. Minutes are to be taken by each person, alternately, and are to be forwarded to me before our next meeting.

We also discussed the revolutionary nature of the actions they were about to embark upon and how a revolution "isn't a dinner party!" They assured me they were ready and able to revolt against the revolting conditions of their family life.

Several days later Carolyn wrote me the following letter:

After our appointment on Friday morning, it wasn't till 3 p.m. that the reason for my servile mentality emerged. I'd like to share it with you; it won't be new to you but it was to me!

Briefly, I was the oldest in a family of four girls and grew up on a farm. My parents were pretty busy and I always felt my mother wasn't too organized so I assumed a lot of responsibilities — the two youngest sisters were 8 and 10 years younger than me and I used to make their lunches, cook their breakfast, plait their hair, sew their dresses, clean the house, weed the garden . . . I even taught my youngest sister to read before she went to school. I was thorough! And the praise I got was wonderful. My mother told her friends: "Carolyn is a real mother; she's my right hand helper, etc." So this was something I was good at! Then I was a primary school teacher for nine years — serving again. And it gave me the skills to serve my children — I was so pleased when Marissa showed an interest in project work and supported her. . . . Then Tony had a drinking problem till last year and from Friday night to Sunday was not available, being either drunk or sleeping off a hangover, so I transferred all my love and attention onto the children. I still have problems in this area and feel insecure about socializing with Tony — how drunk will he get? How can I get him to come home? But this is a separate issue.

Friends have reinforced my servile mentality too — in conversations about what we're doing for our children, I'd be told: "Carolyn, you're such a good mother." If they only knew what I was suffering!

And Marissa's teacher, at an end of year function last year, said: "I am so pleased with Marissa's work — see that she keeps it up." I remember replying: "It's stopping her that's the problem and the demands on me." The teacher looked blank. You can see from the school report the standard I had to maintain.

The following are the dated *secret escape meeting minutes* that Carolyn and Tony have generously agreed to make public:

Friday, 13th

Nothing was said about our appointment with David Epston — Marissa worked on her homework all day — then at 7 p.m., it was as if the reality had dawned on her and she pushed me (Carolyn) up in a corner and screamed: "You're not going to sign that thing. I promise if you help me with this assignment I won't ask you ever again." She was hysterical with rage and thrashed out at me. I took hold of her tightly by the arms and said: "I am, and that's that!" I felt like crying but didn't and had a meeting to go to that evening – normally I'd have felt so drained and unable to face people that I would have phoned to say I couldn't make the meeting. However, several of the women have known about my problem for some time and wanted to know what the outcome of our session with David had been and I felt okay about sharing the truth – for years I've tried to cover up. They're all very supportive and Margaret offered me the use of her cottage at Waiwera should I feel like a couple of days away. The evening ended with a positive statement from everyone – mine had to be that I had at last taken the first step and things were going to be better.

When I got home Tony said Marissa had asked if she could sleep in Mum's bed and Tony said: "No, I'm sleeping with Mum tonight." She went off to bed in her own room.

Saturday, 14th

Marissa came through to me as I was just waking up and said: "Can you take me to the shops, Mum, to buy some cardboard for my project cover?" I said: "I'm not to have anything to do with any aspect of your homework." She said: "Ooh, you can still do that." I thought it was okay to say that I had to go down to the Dominion Road shops anyway and I'd give her some money to buy her own cardboard.

Michael had an outburst over wanting to take a very full bowl of porridge through to the TV room and I said: "No, I don't want you to take that through there – you could spill it on the carpet." He wouldn't listen and carried on with what he wanted to do. So I took the bowl and emptied in into the dog's dish. He was very angry – hit me and threatened me with the tape dispenser; then I smacked his bottom and he went away sadly. He watched TV for a while, then went for a ride on his bike and found a friend who was going to the swimming pool so went off with him. Michael was fine and happy for the rest of the day.

Tony and I had a meeting about plotting ways for Marissa to

work independently on her homework and I told Tony I was still feeling pretty anxious about Marissa not having her project ready to hand in on Monday. At the Parent Teacher Meeting, I'd heard the teacher saying their marks would be penalized if they didn't meet the deadlines. At least I haven't said one word of this worry to Marissa—it's hard. I thought Tony should check with her what work she had left to do and point out just how many hours were left to complete this. Tony agreed. I left Tony and Marissa working together on her homework and walked around the block to ask Rod Hansen to make a legal document releasing me from any responsibility for supporting Marissa's homework lifestyle and handing over the responsibility to Tony. Rod only too happy to oblige.

When I came home Marissa very upset about my having gone out without telling her. I suppose I was away for one hour. And when I told her why I'd gone around to see Rod all hell broke loose! She verbally and physically attacked me for approximately one hour: "I hate adults. I'll pay you all the money in the world if you don't sign that thing. Just don't do it and I promise everything will be happy again. I hate that man we went to see. When I grow up I just want to live in a big house with lots and lots of dogs—no adults. Dad can't help me with my homework—he's dumb. Mum can help me best. I'm going to kill myself. You don't care. You don't love me anymore. You only care about yourself."

It was rough but somewhere I found an inner strength and no way could I change my mind about what I was doing. David said: "Are you ready for a revolution because this is going to be a revolution and revolutions usually mean a lot of pain." Well, this is it!

Sunday, 15th

Marissa up doing her homework before I got out of bed. No good mornings from Marissa—she's feeling cold towards me, which is understandable, but I don't mind—I've got some space! Marissa got her own cereal for breakfast—normally she'd have called out for me to bring it to her and me being afraid of getting in a tizz would obey . . .

Another friend phoned me last night offering the use of a house at Snell's Beach. Marissa heard the conversation and said, "You've told the whole world just so your friends will feel sorry for you." I said, "No, I haven't told the whole world and you get some friends and you'll be able to tell them all your problems." No reply.

Marissa grabbed a felt pen and wrote "Fuck you" over a painted surface in the kitchen — real angry. In the morning I cleaned it off with Ajax, knowing it was her job and that there only needed to be a knock on the door and she'd rush to clean it off. Phil, who is staying with us, noticed that she had tried to clean it off last night. So mid-morning, when Nana knocked on the door, Phil noticed Marissa fly through to the kitchen in a panic to find something to cover it over with and Phil very wisely said that he had cleaned it off.

While talking to Nana, Michael was asking how old the olive tree on the adjoining property might be. Marissa said, "It's not old as Mum. Nothing's older than her." She's got it in for me. I ignored it. Nana reprimanded her.

I went out to visit friends in the afternoon and told Marissa I was going out. She said, "I want to come too." But this time I said: "No, I'm going out alone." Normally, I'd have said, "Okay."

When I got home Tony and Michael were playing chess, Shayne had gone out for a walk with the father and child from next door, and Marissa was doing her homework. She has been cold towards me all day but I don't mind. After dinner she had another outburst of rage and anger — I haven't brought the subject up but it was all about: "I don't want you to sign that thing. You have ruined our happy family. I'll give you all my money if you don't sign that thing. You can sell the TV rather than sign that thing. You have ruined everything. I'm not going back to see that man again; I hate him." She verbally and physically attacked me for about an hour until Tony's daughter, Marilyn, arrived. She slunk off to bed and didn't make another appearance. I went in and kissed her when she was asleep.

Michael also had another outburst — he too is very full of anger. A repeat of yesterday's situation — this time he wanted to take his plate of baked beans through to TV and I said: "No, because if it spills, it stains the carpet." He also attacked me and threw things at me — felt pens. He didn't eat any baked beans and sulked for a while but he went to bed happily.

Monday, 16th

Marissa came out to me in the kitchen and said, "You've made me sick in my stomach." I just said, "Oh." She went off to do more homework, then got her own breakfast—normally she'd have been calling out, "Mum! Get me my breakfast!" and I'd have obliged. I did go out and pick parsley and chives from the garden for her cooking class and packed an egg in tissue paper, which she gathered up and put in a container. No thank you's. She asked Tony to take her to school as she was running late—normally it would have been me! I said, "Can I have a kiss goodbye?" and she walked away but a few minutes later came and kissed me and I kissed her."

I replied to these notes when I received them:

Dear Carolyn and Tony,

Many thanks for your progress notes. Who would have thought that you would have made so much progress so quickly? Marissa's homework lifestyle has lost its main support and I think you can expect to see it losing some of its influence over her. And only then will she be able to make friends among those who do not subscribe to the idea of perfection.

Carolyn, in your letter you have most adequately explained your training in serving others. I hope in the next week or two you might like to reconsider the idea of being for others and consider the idea of being more for yourself. Your life so far has been one of giving; isn't it time you did some taking and others gave back to you?

I would like to commend you both for your courage in initiating a revolution in your family and in your life. No, it won't be easy, but it will be a lot easier than you might anticipate. Also, I can reassure you that your children will be far happier under your new regime.

Keep in touch.

Regards,
D. E.

Further escape meeting notes arrived along with Carolyn's *Declaration of Independence:*

Monday, 16th

Tonight Marissa is working independently on her homework. She has set herself up in the lounge — not in front of the TV in the dining room as usual.

She asked Tony to go and buy her some white-out. I'd already mentioned to Tony earlier that I thought it would be a good idea if she needed white-out, cardboard, glue, etc., she could pay for it out of her $4 pocket money. Tony said, "There's no way I'm going down to the shops at this time." It was 6 p.m. and he had just got home. "How much does it cost?" She said, "$2.00." "How long does it last?" She said, "Six months," but, thinking about it, said, "Four months." The reality is that she's been through a whole bottle since the beginning of Feb. She didn't continue with the request.

Marissa is working independently on her homework; she has been working all evening since 5 p.m. and it's now 8. Kept going till about 10 p.m.

We discussed going out as a family on the weekend and whether or not we should forewarn Marissa of our plans so she can do her homework around this time. I thought it only fair to be advised in advance but Tony disagreed. He felt it was too accommodating of the homework lifestyle.

Wednesday, 18th

Yesterday she was up at 7 a.m. to do homework, got her own breakfast, and walked to school. Tony bought white-out and a magazine she needed for her project. When Tony arrived home Marissa thanked him twice. I drove her to drama class after school and when I collected her she said everyone was sad when the class finished and she'd really enjoyed it.

She worked on homework from 6 to 10 p.m. Tony was in same room by his choice for most of the evening.

Marissa showed Tony the note from her teacher saying, "Don't do this for homework because you're a bit bogged down."

I've made a mistake this morning as she asked me last night to wake her up early in the morning and I did wake her up at 7 a.m. and she said, "I haven't got time for breakfast."

Should we provide an alarm clock? Tony says, "No, she's got to learn to go to bed early enough if she wants to get up early in the morning." He's going to talk about this today with Marissa.

Thursday, 19th

Today Marissa was doing her homework in front of TV. Michael was there also and wriggled the couch she was sitting on and they ended up having a fight. I intervened and told her that she is not to do her homework in front of television. So she took her homework to the porch and set herself up on Michael's bed. Later in the evening Carolyn went to get some notes out of her drawer and found them missing. She knew immediately that Marissa must have taken them. Marissa admitted taking them and said she had burned them but she hadn't. She said, "You will never get them back." She had to move her homework through to her room as Michael wanted to go to bed so I took some of her homework from her and said, "When you give the notes back, you can have your homework back." Then she said, "I don't care about the homework, you're not getting the notes back." I got angry and smacked her, which, on reflection, I should have given her more of a chance to think about it. However, the notes appeared outside her door very quickly. Then I gave her homework back. After that she turned the light off and went to bed. Carolyn then had a good chat with her after that and Marissa cuddled her. I kissed her goodnight and said, "I'm sorry for smacking you," and she said, "Forgiven."

Carolyn also included her *Declaration of Independence*, dated the 6th of the next month:

> When it becomes necessary for anyone to dissolve a problem it is necessary to declare the causes which have impelled them to take action.
> All people are created equal with certain rights including Life, Liberty, and the pursuit of Happiness and when

any situation intervenes where these needs cannot be obtained it is the right of the person to alter or abolish the wrongs and institute a new regime, laying its foundation in such a form to effect their safety and happiness.

But when a long train of abuses of my rights has developed it is my right and duty to throw off such developments and provide a new order of balance. I have been the patient sufferer of my daughter's orders and decided to seek the help of a Family Therapist to alter this situation.

To prove this state of affairs let these facts be submitted: I have had very little time to myself as I have had to be available to help Marissa with her homework. I have had to bring her drinks and food as she has requested them so that she is not interrupted while doing her homework. I have had to purchase excessive paper as in her constant striving for perfection and therefore constant repetition of work, she has used screeds of paper. I have had to take responsibility for seeing that she completes her work to meet deadlines for assignments to be handed in for marking. I have had to pick up books that have fallen off the arm of a chair. I have spent hours assisting Marissa with projects as she has strived to maintain a standard of excellence. After school I have driven to three different libraries to find the correct reference book. I have been uneasy and unrelaxed about going out with Marissa as she would be unable to enjoy herself, complain about being bored, and demand to go home earlier than I desired so that she could do her homework. I have had to stay up late at night to help her with her homework and wake her early in the morning to comfort her as she cried because she hadn't done her homework. If I have been unwell I've been told that I'm always feeling sorry for myself. I have had to witness her aggression, bullying and dominance towards her brother, Michael, should he accidentally stand on a piece of homework or wobble the chair she was sitting on. I have barely tolerated her dislike and complaints of food I have prepared for her: "I won't eat those sandwiches. There are crumbs in the bag you put them in." I have had to listen to constant demands of "Mum." I have had to contend with almost every request being met with a definite "No." I have had to tolerate Marissa's constant rudeness if I've taken too long to meet her requests, e.g., knocking on the front door when the back door is open and being greeted with a sour face and a message: "about time too and *you* can put the key back up on the ledge." I have had to meet her constant demands for affection, especially to comfort her after her tantrums. I have had to be able to withstand her corrections in my conversations with my friends.

I therefore declare that I have a right to my own independence, safety and happiness and uphold the ideal of being more for myself rather than serving others and so release Marissa from the curse of the idea of perfection.

Carolyn Storey

We met one month later as agreed. Marissa arrived wearing sunglasses and was determined not to enter into conversation with me. However, Carolyn and Tony spoke with excitement about the events that had transpired since our first meeting. The following are some excerpts from the transcript of that meeting:

DE: What about you, Tony? How did you find the revolution? It was a short revolution, wasn't it. The lifestyle was overthrown in a matter of two days. How did you experience it?

TONY: Oh, the same as Carolyn. I got angry a couple of times but, well, really angry actually, but it just seemed to pass after a couple of days and things became different.

DE: Could you describe it for us so that other people can be on the lookout?

TONY: I felt very frustrated like the fact that (inaudible) . . . she changed quite a bit.

DE: Could you tell me how she changed just to put other fathers on the lookout so that they will be able to observe the same changes? How did you see her change? Was it in the way she behaved or the way she looked?

TONY: Well, I think lately she is looking better and she is less aggressive and that she accepts things, like if you ask her to do something then she accepts it much better. Just generally her attitude and behavior are much better.

. . . . .

DE: Tony, how have things changed for you and Carolyn now that you are not so busy fighting with Marissa's homework habit?

TONY: We have a better relationship.

DE: There must have been a lot of tension . . .

CAROLYN: It would set Tony and I off against the other because I would think he was interfering when he would try and stop me from being involved.

TONY: Yes, we would end up fighting each other.

DE: I think that is how homework habits rule us — by dividing parents. And you are not being divided by the homework habit anymore?

CAROLYN: Tony keeps asking me to do all these things, like asking me to come and watch this program on TV.

DE: So are you trying to involve Carolyn in your life a bit?

CAROLYN: I'm not used to it so I am floating around a bit . . . I never had time to listen to Tony over the last few months. I was just worn out.

DE: Are you finding that Carolyn and you are getting a bit more connected up because this would have disconnected you in a sense?

TONY: Yes, we are a lot more relaxed. I think so anyway. What about you?

CAROLYN: Yes, much better.

. . . . .

DE: And tell me, was doing your *Declaration of Independence* an important ingredient to your success?

CAROLYN: I think reading it more than writing it because I have been thinking a lot about it anyway, so it probably was. I don't know if I have written it all that well but I think it was good for me to write down all those things, all the reasons why we came to you in the first place, just to recall those things.

Carolyn and Tony also donated with good humor an article entitled "Please Sir . . . I Did My Best," written by Dorothy Coup, from the *New Zealand Herald*. Coup writes:

Later come projects. And how we parents love projects —
taking the children to the library, looking up encyclope-
dias and searching out information and pictures. "How did
you get on with your son's last project?" is a common topic
of conversation among friends with children in the same
class. "Oh, I got an A." "Very good. We got only a B plus,
but I had a lot of meetings that week." "Well, I got Karl to
get an extension for his project for another week because I
got the flu." Only the most neglectful parents would think
of letting their children do a project alone.

They thought other families might find this useful, and, in fact,
this has been the case.

I phoned one month later to find that Marissa was no longer
worrying about studying or repeating her work and crossing out.
There had been no further difficulties between her and her brother. Carolyn was finding it hard to get over her incredulity but was
now regretting she hadn't taken action sooner. Marissa had
stopped complaining about her signing "that thing," and Carolyn
couldn't remember when she last did so. The marital relationship
had improved, and the family now was able to go on outings and
had done so twice within the last month.

Several weeks later, after some discussion, Carolyn agreed to act
as consultant to the Jones family. Carolyn arranged to meet with
Mrs. Jones and tell her about their family's revolution (see Epston,
1989).

Nine months later Carolyn summarized:

*It's hard to remember what Marissa was like . . . how terrible
things were. It's unbelievable how different things are. She still
does her homework but it doesn't matter if she doesn't finish
things; whereas before, I couldn't get her to go to bed before 11
and then she would wake up crying at 7. She's not uptight about it
any longer. She and her brother are good friends now. They spend
quite a lot of time together sitting and talking. They felt together
because I had done something about Marissa and I had taken
them to see you. Their friendship developed gradually. Before,*

Marissa was full of hate for her brother and me, blaming me if her work wasn't finished on time. Her brother got it for anything at all. She then turned her resentment on her father but that is okay now. She can now accept things instead of swearing at me. . . . I had to tread on tender ground. She is very, very different. She is more relaxed and more outgoing. She's made other friends, stays overnight, and went to a school camp. She wouldn't have done that before because she would have been worried about eating different foods. She used to be obsessed that I be around all the time. She is catching up on all the play she has missed out on for years. She is being normal and a human being. She's definitely happier; before, she was so full of worry, crying, tantrumming, and worn out. She is no longer critical of herself—nothing was ever right about her. She stopped excessive washing in the bathroom and of her feet and sandals. That's just stopped. I feel tremendous. It was hard the first few days. But soon, everything seemed so much lighter. I've been able since then to face other problems in my life. It's been a cleansing year. I was hiding behind the problem with Marissa. I was scared to go out as she had started kicking me in public because she wanted to go home. It's the opposite now—she wants to stay out.

The relationship between Tony and me has improved. We used to blame each other for Marissa's problems. I am reaching out to friends; before, I was hiding from them.

Carolyn contacted the school regarding her concerns. As a result, when Marissa's school had an awards-giving day at the end of the academic year, Marissa was called up to the stage and granted a special prize for her "unobtrusive participation in class activities and her caring for others." Marissa modestly accepted her award.

4. Counter Documents

If, in our world, language plays a very central part in those activities that define and construct persons, and if written language makes a more than significant contribution to this, then a consideration of modern documents and their role in the redescription of persons is called for.

The proliferation and elevated status of the modern document are reflected by the fact that it is increasingly relied upon for a variety of decisions about the worth of persons. For example, in job applications it is standard practice for the documents that are available on the person to be reviewed before the person is interviewed, and there exist circumstances in which decisions are wholly made about the applicant's worth, not through a meeting of persons, but through a meeting of documents. Thus, documents have become influential in the lives of persons to the extent that they precede and preclude persons in a great number of situations.

In the domain of the professional disciplines, a document can be seen to serve several purposes, not the least of which is the presentation of the "self" of the subject of the document and of its author. The subject of most professional documents is a person who submits to, or has been submitted for, evaluation, and the author of the document is a person skilled in the rhetoric pertaining to a specific domain of expert knowledge. This person has, at his/her disposal, a library of terms of description that have been invented by and are considered the property of this particular domain of expert knowledge. These terms of description "specify the subject" of the document.

These documents have an existence independent of their author and their subject. In researching psychiatry's practice of "file-speak," Harre (1985), in referring to the way that the psychiatric

188

document—more specifically, the file—has a life of its own, states: "A file has an existence and a trajectory through the social world, which soon takes it far outside the reach of its subject" (p. 179).

The life of the file proceeds through the process of "retranscription," and in this process the patient's experience is appropriated and transferred into the domain of expert knowledge. The language of the patient is transcribed into "official language," everyday descriptions of problems into correct diagnoses—from "feeling miserable" to "displays low affect." Eventually the patient's experience is not recognizable within the terms of its original presentation. In studying just two steps in this retranscription process, steps that relate to the exchange of letters between consultants about the patient, Harre observes:

> . . . the two processes of transcription inserted into the trajectory of the file formed a kind of dispersion in which the meaning of the complaint was essentially lost. In returning to the language of the patient after the two transcriptions, it was often difficult to identify traces of the original complaint. (p. 179)

In addition to the role of the modern document in the redescription and presentation of the self of its subject, it has another role that is perhaps more primary in many circumstances. This is the presentation of the self of its author. Documents are shaped by a rhetoric, and this rhetoric serves to establish, in the reader, "a certain impression of the character and the moral qualities of the . . . writer in a given situation" (Harre, 1985). Thus, documents are a vehicle for the presentation and display of the author's worth according to moral criteria that have been established in a particular discipline. And in so doing, such documents shape the author's life as they do the subject's.

In scientistic disciplines the rhetoric is such that it establishes the author's worth through creating the impression of the possession of an objective and detached view. Here, the demonstration of adequate knowledge of the relevant library of facts—for example, the psychiatric library of descriptions for problems-in-persons—and of "diagnostic acumen" is a foremost mechanism of the author's "claims of honor," critical to the achievement of esteem in the eyes of this professional community.

Psychiatry is by no means the only discipline that employs the file for the redescription of persons and for the presentation of the moral worth of the author. All of the disciplines have requirements of self-presentation and, according to Foucault (1979), the rise and spectacular success of all the disciplines have been entirely facilitated by those practices of evaluation (normalizing judgment) and documentation that enable the subjugation of persons.

In studying the history of the ascription of problematic identity to persons and the separation of those persons from the population at large, Foucault referred to the emergence of the "dividing practices" or the "practices of exclusion" (1965, 1973). In the light of this analysis, we can consider the very significant part that documents, such as the file, play in modern 'rituals of exclusion.'*

However, not all of the cultural practices that employ a documentation of the redescription of persons do so within the context of the disciplines, and not all of these practices marginalize persons by presenting an image of the "spoiled identity" of the document's subject. There are those practices, situated in the domain of alternative local, popular knowledges, that have the capacity to redescribe and specify persons in ways that emphasize their special knowledges and competencies, as well as their place in the larger community of persons. The bestowing of awards is one example of these practices.

The practices associated with these alternative documents contrast with those associated with file. Whereas the file has a narrow readership of professional experts, the news carried by the award is more widely available to the community. Whereas the file has a significant, if not central, part in rituals of exclusion, the award is more often associated with what Bryan Turner (Turner & Hepworth, 1982) refers to as "rituals of inclusion."

Awards of various kinds, such as trophies and certificates, can

---

*Compare Garfinkel's (1956) "Conditions of Successful Degradation Ceremonies" and Goffman's (1961) *Asylums*, pp. 117–156.

be considered examples of alternative documents.* Such awards often signal the person's arrival at a new status in the community, one that brings with it new responsibilities and privileges. As these alternative documents have the potential of incorporating a wide readership and of recruiting an audience to the performance of new stories, they can be situated in what Myerhoff (1982) refers to as definitional ceremonies:

> I have called such performances "Definitional Ceremonies," understanding them to be collective self-definitions specifically intended to proclaim an interpretation to an audience not otherwise available. (p. 105)

The incorporation of a wider readship and the recruitment of an audience contribute not just to the survival and consolidation of new meanings, but also to a revision of the preexisting meanings.

There are also those documents that are significantly authored by the person who is their subject. In these documents, the subject plays a central role in contributing to the specification of her own self. In so doing, she becomes conscious of her participation in the constitution of her own life. This can lead to a profound sense of personal responsibility, as well as, a sense of possessing the capacity to intervene in the shaping of one's life and relationships. In a similar vein, Myerhoff (1982), in referring to the self-presentational and self-constitutional activities of an aging Jewish community in Venice, California, observes that they:

> . . . assume responsibility for inventing themselves and yet maintain their sense of authenticity and integrity. Such people exercise power over their images, in their own eyes and to some extent in the eyes of whoever may be observing them. Sometimes the image is the only part of their lives subject to control. But this is not a small thing to control. It may lead to a realization of personal power and

---

*However, we do understand that even these can be specifying according to the dominant knowledges.

serve as a source of pleasure and understanding in the workings of consciousness. (p. 100)

CERTIFICATES

In the following pages, various documents that celebrate the new story are represented. For example, we have included a sample of the awards that we have co-constructed with the persons to whom they refer. Readers will notice a progression in the development of these, with the later certificates more explicitly inviting ongoing performances of meaning on behalf of the recipient and the audience to this award. On many occasions, the recipients of these awards have enthusiastically recruited audiences that were not referred to in therapy. For example, we have found children taking fear-busting certificates to school and endeavoring to identify other children who either are in need of assistance or might already be members of the Fear Tamers and Monster Catchers Association.

DECLARATIONS

A Declaration of Independence *

Daniel, aged 14, developed asthma at the age of 10. This was first recognized as exercise-induced wheezing. When he presented to Auckland Hospital for the first time in September 1984, unstable chronic asthma was diagnosed. He was admitted to hospital for one month and subsequently followed up by the pediatric asthma clinic. In September of 1986, Daniel was admitted because of an acute, severe asthma attack that was life-threatening. He was referred for family therapy in April 1987 due to the continuing instability of his asthma control, despite the best efforts of his parents and a family doctor. He was on what was regarded as maximal drug therapy for chronic asthma at his age. The concern

*Co-authored by Innes Asher (Senior Lecturer in Pediatrics, University of Auckland) and David Epston.

Dulwich Centre

345 Carrington Street,
Adelaide, South Australia. 5000
Phone: (08) 223 3966

Monster-Tamer & Fear-Catcher Certificate

This is to certify that

....

has undergone a Complete Training Programme in Monster-Taming and Fear-Catching, is now a fully qualified Monster-Tamer and Fear-Catcher, and is available to offer help to other children who are bugged by fears.

dated the ....day of ....19......

Signed: ....

Michael White
President,
Monster-Taming & Fear-Catching
Association of Australia.

𝔅eating 𝔖neaky 𝔚ee ℭertificate

This certificate is granted to _____ in recognition of his success at putting Sneaky Wee in its proper place.

_____ has turned the tables on Sneaky Wee. Sneaky Wee was running out on him. Now he has run out on Sneaky Wee. Instead of soaking in Sneaky Wee, he is soaking in glory.

Awarded on the _____ day of _____

𝔖igned: _____

𝔐ichael 𝔚hite

Breaking the Grip of Sneaky Poo
Certificate

This certificate is awarded to _____ for taking his life out of
the grip of "Sneaky Poo". Now Sneaky Poo is in ____'s grip, and he
can put Sneaky Poo where it belongs.

Sneaky Poo was messing up ____'s life, and often gave him a really
hard time by sticking around when it wasn't wanted. Sneaky Poo even
tried to trick ____ into believing that it was his playmate.

Now that ____ doesn't have a messed up life, Sneaky Poo can't give
him a hard time and can't trick him any longer. Anybody who would like to
know how ____ took his life out of the grip of Sneaky Poo can ask him
some questions.

Congratulations ____ !

Awarded on the ____ day of _____1989

Signed: _____

Michael White

𝕮𝖊𝖗𝖙𝖎𝖋𝖎𝖈𝖆𝖙𝖊 𝖔𝖋 𝕮𝖔𝖓𝖈𝖊𝖓𝖙𝖗𝖆𝖙𝖎𝖔𝖓

This certificate is awarded to _____ *for taking charge of, and strengthening, his concentration. In achieving this, he has noticed that he has become more popular with himself.*

_____ did so well at strengthening his concentration that he even surprised himself. When other people also get surprised at how much_____ can now do for himself, reading this certificate will help them understand what has happened.

Awarded on the _____ *day of* _____

𝕾𝖎𝖌𝖓𝖊𝖉: _____

𝕸𝖎𝖈𝖍𝖆𝖊𝖑 𝖂𝖍𝖎𝖙𝖊

𝔈scape 𝔉rom 𝔗antrums 𝔈ertificate

This certificate is to let everyone know that _____ has escaped from tantrums. These tantrums were really playing up and giving him and other people a very hard time.

_____ will be happy to tell people about how he taught the tantrums a very important lesson. Now the tantrums know that he will not put up with them giving him or anyone else a hard time.

Three cheers for _____!

Presented on the _____ day of _____

𝔖igned: _____   _____

          𝔐ichael 𝔚hite   &   _____

𝕰𝖘𝖈𝖆𝖕𝖊 𝕱𝖗𝖔𝖒 𝕸𝖎𝖘𝖊𝖗𝖞 𝕮𝖊𝖗𝖙𝖎𝖋𝖎𝖈𝖆𝖙𝖊

This certificate is awarded to _____ in recognition of her success in turning her back on misery and walking away from it.

She has deprived misery of her company with the full knowledge that misery loves company, and in fact feeds on company.

This certificate will serve to remind _____, and others that she is the sort of person that is more suited to happiness than to misery.

Awarded on the _____ day of _____

𝕾𝖎𝖌𝖓𝖊𝖉: _____

𝕾𝖎𝖌𝖓𝖊𝖉: _____

𝕸𝖎𝖈𝖍𝖆𝖊𝖑 𝖂𝖍𝖎𝖙𝖊

Escape From Guilt Certificate

This certificate is awarded to _____ in recognition of her victory over guilt.

Now that guilt doesn't have such a priority in her life, she is able to give herself a priority in her own life. Now that she is not guilt's person, she is free to be her own person.

This certificate will serve to remind _____, and others, that she has resigned from the position of super-responsibility in the lives of others, and that she is no longer vulnerable to invitations from others to have their life for them and to put her life to one side.

Awarded on the _____ day of _____

Signed: _____

_____

Signed: _____

Michael White

𝕨inning 𝔸gainst 𝔹ad ℍabits ℭertificate

*This certificate is presented to _____ because he did very
well at stopping bad habits from pushing him around.*

*Because he now knows so much about winning against bad
habits, any child who wants help in getting rid of bad habits
could ask _____ for help.*

*Every time that _____ walks past this certificate he will get
proud of himself. Every time that other people walk past this
certificate they will realize how well he did.*

Congratulations _____!

Awarded on the _____ day of _____

𝔖igned: _____

                    𝔐ichael 𝔚hite

𝔚itnessed: _____

                    _____

Diploma Of Special Knowledge

This is to proclaim that in the year _____ identified and felt entitled to embrace her own special knowledge of her children's needs and of the requirements to enrich their futures.

Further, it has been acknowledged by all those who have been fortunate enough to witness this achievement, that her success has required extraordinary effort in the face of considerable adversity.

The fact that _____ has become an advisor to herself heralds her arrival at a more accepting relationship with herself in which she can more fully appreciate her own wisdom.

This diploma is bestowed in recognition of _____ achievement and so that those who were unable to witness her success at claiming her own special knowledge may develop some understanding of the changes they are noticing in the _____ family.

This diploma also gives notice that _____ is prepared for and would welcome questions from others like:

"It's really refreshing to see that you now feel able to take more of your own advice. How is it that you have been able to come home to yourself?"

"How is it that you came to trust your own authority and to depend upon it more than the authority of others?"

"Now that you have the opportunity to practice your own problem-solving ability in your own life, what difference is this making to the future of your family?"

This diploma is active from the ____ day of _____

Signed: _____   Signed: _____

Michael White

was that, in the face of this instability, he might have a further life-threatening attack. This needed to be prevented at all costs.

Daniel looked much younger than his age and found it odd to be asked direct questions. He would seek assistance of either his mother or his father in answering such questions. When I asked him what his understanding of asthma was he seemed somewhat puzzled by the question and had to admit that he didn't know. To the complementary question, "If asthma-watching was 100%, how much asthma-watching do you (Daniel) do, and how much asthma-watching do your parents do?" Daniel once again found himself unable to answer and referred the question to his parents. I requested that he persist until he discovered his own answer. He ended up shaking his head quizzically. By now his parents were laughing as they knew the answer only too well: "We asthma-watch 99% and he watches 1%." I then asked his parents if Daniel was, by nature, trusting, unsuspecting, and natural. They agreed with me that he was.

Externalizing asthma as a trickster, dependent on deviousness and cunning, I asked questions about his experience of asthma. This resulted in descriptions of him as a person who was inattentive, off-guard, and ambushed. He became very engaged in the conversation as he started to perceive the injustice of his situation. He reported that he did know what to do, even though he had received instruction from his older sister (Tara, aged 22), who had also suffered from asthma. I relabeled her advice as "mind control."

Daniel's parents then informed me of their frustration with his inability to manage his medication regime and his failure to regularly record his peak flow scores. Questions drew out the relationship between their increasing reliability and his increasing reliance on them. However, given that his life was at stake, they could hardly afford to take any risks. The following letter summarizes a new description, with the requirements of asthma control taking on novel significance.

Dear Jackie, Arthur, and Daniel,

It seemed to us, Daniel, that your asthma is a particularly devious and cunning sort of asthma. By contrast, you appeared to me to be an open, natural, unsuspecting, and trusting young person. When you are sick, you give in to your asthma as you ought to, but when you are well it seems that you do not keep your guard up, keep on the alert, etc. So, when you finally become aware that asthma is sneaking up on you, it already has a grip on you. To some extent, you have been ambushed. No wonder your mother and father have had to work so hard asthma-watching. Daniel, it's almost as if, when you go against asthma, you make your appearance at half-time and by then you are down 10 goals. It is not surprising that it's too late for you to use your mind control on it, to go on to the offensive against it by "coming inside, sitting down, and relaxing." Tara taught you this and it works, but only when you provide yourself with advance warning. You have come to depend on your parents to provide you with this but they have to depend on you to provide them with some warning. Peak flows are your main means of detection.

We agreed on the following plan of action:

1. Instead of forgetting about your asthma and getting back into your normal routine, Daniel, you agreed to increase your cunning and watchfulness. The other possibility was to try to talk asthma into becoming less devious and more respectful of your growing up, but we all decided that there wasn't much hope in that. Your asthma plays dirty and, if you want to reduce your dependence on prednisone, you will have to learn to out-trick a trickster by developing counter-tricks of your own. You agreed, Daniel, to go on a spying mission against asthma in order to learn its ways and means. This, of course, is only a first step. You thought that the best way to do this was the following: take six peak flows per day and carefully record your scores in a secret notebook that you keep hidden on your person. The chart on the fridge should be taken down. Jackie and Arthur, if you become worried, Daniel permits you to ask him to check his book. Daniel, you are also to jot down any of asthma's tricks if asthma tries to make a comeback against you. Daniel, if you fail yourself, your parents will have to take over from you.

2. *This experiment has another side to it. Daniel, you agreed to take over responsibility for self-medication and to stop inviting your parents by your trusting nature to do it for you. The purpose of this experiment is for you to learn more about your friends (medicines), which, of course, are your asthma's enemies.*

3. *You are to have an appointment with Dr. Asher all by yourself. Your job is to ask her questions about the side effects of a dependence on prednisone and your other medications. Before you go, you are to make up a list of questions all by yourself so you won't forget anything.*

> *Good luck!*
> *D. E.*

Daniel's parents could not attend the next meeting one month later as his mother had been rushed to hospital. Sadly, she was diagnosed as suffering from a life-threatening illness. She now had her own fight to fight, and we discussed this over the phone. However, Daniel arrived with a plastic bag full of asthma pamphlets he had been consulting following his meeting with Dr. Asher. He was far more authoritative, even though he had had a three-day admission. He had taken over full responsibility for his medication and had zealously taken and recorded his peak flows.

Dear Daniel,

Daniel, you certainly are studying up on asthma. As you put it, "I've got a better view of what drugs are doing, what good relaxing is . . . like it makes you able to breathe better." I was interested to see the books you are readings and wonder if you have embarked upon an asthma-expert career. When you meet Denise Gordon*, you will be taking another step or two in this direction. Daniel, if

---

*Asthma Educator, Auckland Public Hospital.

you become more expert in asthma, your asthma will no longer be able to make a fool of you.

Daniel, you cut down on your admission time from two weeks to three days. You took your inhaler regularly and stopped forgetting. Daniel, as you put it, you are playing the full game and are certainly scoring more goals against asthma than asthma is scoring against you. And your asthma watchfulness is "a load off my parents' minds." Asthma no longer can push you over with a feather. You said that asthma would think this of you: "That guy's more alert: I'm going to have to try harder to out-trick him." Of course, you have some counter-tricks up your sleeve. You have been keeping your secret diary: "I can keep an eye on it (asthma) and map its activities—it tells me where it's up to." And you hit the highest peak flow: 470. No wonder you are so full of pride: "I got better quick—three days instead of two weeks."

No doubt asthma still has a few more tricks to try out on you so you will still have to keep on-guard.

With all this in mind, no wonder your Mum and Dad are so pleased that you did what you said you'd do.

You suggested some experiments:

1. *acquire some more asthma knowledge and better learn its ways and means;*
2. *keep up your current level of asthma-watching and self-medication;*
3. *experiment with relaxing so you get the little ones so no big ones create themselves;*
4. *more map-reading so in the end you will break asthma's code.*

I look forward to meeting with you again. So far, you tell me you have increased your self-pride by "heaps," "a lot," "70%." Will you improve upon that improvement?

D. E.

Daniel, his father, and I met six weeks later. They had responded well to a drop in Daniel's peak flow readings according to their "crisis plan." Daniel spontaneously had hit upon the idea of a science project on asthma. The following letter summarizes the meeting:

Dear Arthur, Jackie, and Daniel,

Daniel, you have continued keeping up with your alertness to asthma's tricks of the trade. By doing so, you were able to notice "a drop" in your peak flows, start corrective measures quickly, and more or less pull out of it before you were out of control. Arthur, you said that "we got on to his inhaler quickly" and "got on to his prednisone, but got off it quickly before it got hold of him," Daniel, you have continued your asthma-watching and, as you put it, Arthur: "We are keeping out of it." Daniel, you have also continued your asthma-expert career and are feeling more knowledgeable. Before you were asthma-innocent. I thought it was an inspired move to undertake your research project on asthma and my guess is that there will be many more learnings to come. Already, your asthma expertise includes the following:

> *(a) I can know what can cause asthma;*
> *(b) I can know what can prevent it; and*
> *(c) I can know about its tricks.*

You tell me that you have increased your asthma knowledge by 50%. You say you feel more grown up "not having to rely on my Mum and Dad so much." I was not at all surprised, Arthur, when you pointed out that Daniel now is also "better with his homework." He is not supervising himself. He has gone from a supervised person to a more self-supervising person. Daniel, I was pretty impressed by the advice you gave yourself: "It just has to be done so I did it." Daniel, your "map reading" of asthma's movements is paying off. You are now catching asthma before it mounts a major attack on you. No wonder your self-pride has increased 20–30% since I last met with you.

Daniel, you agreed to assume responsibility for undertaking the following tasks:

1. to experiment with your sister's ideas on relaxing; and

2. to go to a library and look up a book on American history. Find a copy of the Declaration of Independence *and write your own* Declaration of Independence *from the rule of asthma.*

I look forward to meeting you all again. Jackie, I missed seeing you and I want to pass on my sincere good wishes for your recovery and my respect for your obvious courage.

D. E.

We met six weeks later. My colleague, Paraire Huata*, joined me for this session. Daniel's asthma project had absorbed him and the result was so accomplished that it was entered in the school competition. There was another brief admission to hospital, lasting four days. He had continued to be responsible for his self-medication, peak flow readings, and his school work. Most importantly, he had undertaken the *Declaration of Independence* task. I took this to be extremely demanding and requiring of great perseverence: reading the original, then the exegesis, and then applying it to his personal circumstances. When he read it to me aloud, the document's own rhetoric took him over and I listened spellbound to the compelling nature of his address. The following is the letter describing this meeting:

Dear Daniel, Jackie, and Arthur,

Daniel, you have certainly advanced yourself in your asthma-expert career. Your asthma project was of such a high standard that it went on to the school science exhibition. Your asthma knowledge must be getting "deep," whereas before it was just on the surface. Doing the project gave you plenty of opportunities to absorb and revise your knowledge and I believe that you now know more than you know you know. I suspect this will become apparent to you as time goes by.

---

*Therapist of Leslie Centre.

You did have one admission lasting four days. But remember, you usually spent two weeks in hospital. This was a 65% improvement. Arthur, you said: "It did sneak up on us . . . he went down for a couple of days . . . he deteriorated quickly." Daniel, you said the reason for your 65% improvement was that: "before I wouldn't have been watching it (my asthma) myself." Arthur, you say that Daniel "lets his guard down every so often." Well, no-one's perfect!

Daniel, you reported a new asthma learning: "Sometimes I think I'm better before I'm better. I don't quite get the job done before I want to return to a 'normal' life."

Daniel, I wanted you to ask yourself this question: "Has asthma shrunk my head? Does asthma not want me to really hear it when I'm praised because I might get too strong for it? Would I prefer shrunkenness or self-expansion? Which is the best course in life for me? What would asthma prefer: a shrunken person or a self-expanding person?"

I was very impressed by your Declaration of Independence, a copy of which I have included for you. It really ought to be framed and put above your bed or desk so you can read it at will.

Daniel, according to your Dad, you have continued on your self-supervising course, in regard to both your homework and your asthma ("he's pretty good on his homework").

I ask you to ask yourself this question, too: "If you wait until you get wheezy before you practice your relaxation, do you think you will get very good at it? If a soccer team waited until a big game before it practiced, do you think it would win much?"

Paraire said he wanted you to know that his head didn't swell but his heart did. He wanted me to thank you for sharing your new learnings about yourself with him. What made his heart swell was all the hope and conviction in your Declaration of Independence.

Yours sincerely,
D. E.

Declaration of Independence

When in the course of human events, it becomes necessary for a person to dissolve the bonds which have connected them with asthma, and to assure among the powers of the earth, the separate and equal station to which the laws of nature and of nature's God entitle them to a decent, able life like all others, without having to be watchful of asthma. We hold these truths to be self-evident, that all men are created equal, that they are endowed by their creator with certain inalienable rights, among these are life, liberty from asthma and all other evil things and the pursuit of happiness. And so doctors and medicines are here to protect us. People have the right to change doctors or to try other methods of treatment but people should not make a revolutionary change in long-established doctors, medicines or other things which are working. But they should have the right to overthrow medicines, doctors or other things if they aren't working, or they should have the right to overthrow asthma if it is being evil. So I am doing this. I will overthrow asthma and come under my own rule and choose what I think right for me and not what asthma sees as right. And I will not do anything which inconveniences me that asthma chooses. Asthma has done bad things and causes a lot of inconveniences to us.

So it is with pleasure then that I will from this moment on be rid of asthma rule and shall be free from all its ties.

Daniel Brady _____
declared this on the _____ (day)
of the _____ (month) of 1987
in the city of _____
New Zealand.

This declaration was witnessed by his mother — Jackie
Brady _____
and his father — Arthur Brady _____

Daniel, his father, and I met once again nine weeks later. Daniel had faced his dilemma: self-expansion versus being shrunken by asthma and favored the former as his chosen lifestyle. This session saw him abandon his status of "client" and take upon himself the role of counselor to other young asthma-ruled people.

Dear Daniel, Jackie, and Arthur,

Daniel, you continued your asthma-expert career. People asked you questions about your asthma project and "most of the time I had the answers." And your Mum and Dad were so confident about your asthma-watching that they left you behind and traveled to Christchurch. And you and Tara coped with an asthma emergency and came through with flying colors. In the old days, you very likely would have given up and caved in but now, instead, "because of my notebook," you are "getting on and doing it quick."

With regard to a self-expanding or a shrinking lifestyle, you appear to have chosen self-expansion. The evidence for this is as follows:

> *1. You went on to the offensive against asthma when your parents were away.*
> *2. In the Eastern Bay's school run, Arthur, you reported that Daniel "got wheezy part-way through and kept on running . . . he ran through his wheezing," and by doing so improved his time by a minute and 22 seconds.*
> *3. You are getting stronger in your body and have expanded your height by 3 cm, and your weight by 1kg.*

Your advice to the person you were six months ago was as follows:

> *1. "Keeping the notebook is the main thing . . . and I'm doing it myself." Arthur, you added that Daniel is doing more than just keeping a notebook. He is also "interpreting it."*
> *2. "Learn and study about asthma . . . I learned to run through my wheezing."*
> *3. "Taking early action," and*
> *4. "Learn about yourself." Daniel, by doing so, you say you "have a bit more confidence" and you gained this "by doing things by myself and succeeding."*

Daniel, I wonder if you are ready to start counseling. In order to test your suitability, I proposed you answer the following questions, write them down, and send them to me for assessment:

1. *Who is the better asthma-watcher—you or your parents?*
2. *"Should young people live under the rule of asthma, or should they declare their independence from asthma's domination of their lives?*
3. *If young persons wanted to know what their asthma was up to, how would they find out?*

Arthur, you noticed that Daniel has had a burst of maturing. "He's more independent . . . seems to handle things fairly well . . . cuts his own lunch now . . . does his paper route, and keeps his pushbikes in repair." I, too, noticed that Daniel has had a leap in his growing up.

Daniel, if you had surrendered fully to the rule of asthma, you would have become a shrunken person rather than an expanding person, a weaker person rather than a stronger person, a dependent person rather than an independent person, a hopeless person rather than a hopeful person, a less proud person rather than a proud person, an ill-informed person rather than an informed person, and a less mature person rather than a maturing person. It is clear to me, Daniel, that you are becoming more and more independent from the rule of asthma.

I suggest we meet again in three months' time regarding anti-asthma counseling.

Fond regards,
D. E.

In the 11 months since his referral for family therapy, Daniel has shown some improvement in his asthma control. There have been no further life-threatening asthma attacks. He has been admitted to hospital on two occasions for acute attacks but the severity of asthma on admission has lessened compared to the two admissions before referral. Daniel has managed several asthma attacks at home without admission to hospital. His attitude toward the surveillance of his asthma at a time when he has been under extraordinary stress due to his mother's illness has been excellent.

While Daniel's chronic asthma persists in causing recurrent attacks, his ability to manage these attacks and keep in control of the situation has definitely improved.

SELF-CERTIFICATION

During my first meeting with Louise and her family, I (M. W.) had great difficulty making contact with her. She was quite withdrawn, and any attempt to engage her in conversation provoked a flood of tears. As the interview progressed, she became more distressed, despite all assurances that she ws not required to participate actively. Other members of her family assured me that I was not responsible for Louise's distress, and that this was a common response to any new situation.

Louise was referred to me some years ago with a diagnosis of schizophrenia. She had retired from life at the age of 16 years. She rarely ventured outside the family home, was frequently distressed, became desperate when her parents' reassurance was not constantly available, and was plagued by obsessions and "voices."* When eliciting information about what was of concern to family members, I discovered that they were well versed in Louise's diagnosis and prognosis. They presented me with a rather dismal picture. Everyone seemed entirely oppressed by Louise's schizophrenia. I introduced questions that invited family members to externalize schizophrenia, and encouraged them to relate those matters of immediate concern (see White, 1987).

Towards the end of the meeting, Louise recovered some composure and offered a minimal comment about the effect of schizophrenia on her life. After a break for a team discussion,** I returned to share some of our observations with the family. Special reference was made to our admiration for Louise's comeback against schizophrenia during the meeting, which was all the more

---

*Referred to in the professional domain as "auditory hallucinations."
**Glenside Hospital Family Therapy Unit.

remarkable considering the fact that this had taken place in circumstances that were unfamiliar to her—where she was on shaky ground. In response to questions about how she had achieved this, Louise seemed surprised to discover that this was a significant achievement.

This unique outcome, along with family members' participation in the performance of meaning in relation to it, marked a turning point for Louise and her family. The door was now open for new developments in their lives. Over several sessions, she and other members of her family were invited to participate in the development of a new account of Louise's life and in new descriptions of her as a person and of her relationships. Over this time, Louise escaped her early retirement and developed a thirst for life. Her medication was reduced to a very minimal level as she began to develop a friendship network and took up "voluntary" work.

Over the last few years Louise has continued to have very occasional contact with the team. At these times, she usually calls distressed, complaining that her voices are again getting the better of her and terrorizing her in various ways. An immediate appointment is always offered, and it is usually discovered that Louise has attempted a rather ambitious step before she has sufficiently prepared herself for such a step, that she has attempted to go too far out on a limb "before the limb has grown strong enough to support her out there." (The strength of such limbs is derived from many small stories of success.)

Louise is most vulnerable to such recklessness when she is subjecting herself to certain specifications for personhood that blind her to important aspects of her own unique story about herself. These problematic specifications are often masked as "expectations" and "ambitions," and Louise identifies them in this way. On the occasions that her expectations and ambitions get the upper hand against her better judgment, she experiences her body as a "thing" over which she has no control.

On one such occasion of crisis, Louise called and informed me that she had been given a very hard time by her voices for over two weeks. We coordinated over times, and when I met her in the waiting room she was sobbing. However, on entering the interviewing room she became less distressed and was able to respond to some questions. Yes, she was surprised that she had got herself to the meeting even though the voices had tried to turn her back and had been saying terrible things about me and the team. Yes, it did tell her some things about herself that it was important for her to know—that she could beat the voices even in such circumstances of adversity. Yes, it probably did tell me and my colleagues something that we could appreciate, perhaps that she was stronger than the voices.

As her voices ceased tantrumming,* we discovered that they had attempted to take advantage of Louise when she had stretched herself too far by participating in an ambitious and strenuous work preparation program. Would it be possible for her to appreciate herself without siding with these expectations for herself? "Yes." And did she have some ideas about how she might prove this to her voices? "Yes," she did. During the course of this meeting, when responding to my questions about why the voices were getting so petty in their accusations about her, Louise "pulled the rug out from under the feet of the voices": "Obviously this proves I have weakened them, that they are grasping at straws."

At the end of the session Louise and I put together the following "To Whom It May Concern" letter:

This is to let everybody know that Louise is now a person to suit herself and has her own mind about things. She is the director of her own life and, tantrum as the voices might, there is no way that they can succeed at getting her in the corner. Louise clearly has the upper hand and will continue to do what is necessary to teach the voices a lesson. This does not mean that the voices still won't try to change Louise to suit them. However, we can see that the writing is on the wall for the voices, and Louise has reduced them to silliness. Louise has turned the tables on them and got them on the run. They have been reduced to absurdity, trying to pick on the most ridiculous things imaginable. This proves that they have already been weakened very much by Louise's action.

Further, Louise has recently taken new steps to put the voices

---

*I have often referred to auditory hallucinations as "tantrumming ideas."

Diploma Of Special Knowledge

This certificate is awarded to _____ in recognition of her success at winning back her own life.

She took back her own life even though the voices tried to bluff her into believing that it was their life.

Anyone who reads this certificate will be curious as to how _____ "turned the tables" on the voices, and she is now ready to answer any questions about this.

Whenever the voices read this certificate they will understand that their "number is up".

Signed: _____

_____

Signed: _____

Michael White

(for & on behalf of the team)

in their place. Knowing that the voices try to trick her when she is stretched or worrying too much about others, Louise has been teaching her ambition that she can appreciate herself when she is doing just what she wants to do and at her own pace, and has decided to be more generous with worry. She is going to share the worry around a bit more so that she doesn't put others out of a job and, from now on, will do just her share of the worry. She will even trick the voices into believing that she doesn't worry at all, by helping the people who need her help very slowly.

Whenever the voices are getting loud and unruly, Louise will reduce them to thoughts by holding this letter up in front of them. She will show them no mercy at these times.

Louise departed from the meeting having reduced the voices to quiet thoughts and quite sure that the letter would be effective in assisting her to combat them should they again attempt to take advantage of her. A follow-up meeting was scheduled for two weeks later, and at this review Louise reported that the voices had been much more respectful of her, and that she only had to confront them with the letter on a couple of occasions. They had responded immediately and had stopped hassling her.

Louise continued to make progress, with crises becoming less frequent. When she believed she was ready, the team organized a small party, and together we celebrated and awarded her a diploma of "special knowledge."

CONCLUSION

We have decided to be brief in our concluding remarks as we believe that the various correspondences, letters, documents, and certificates that we have selected for inclusion in this book speak well enough for themselves. This selection has been made with the aim of demonstrating the applicability of literate means to a wide range of presenting problems.

Jerome Bruner rests his case for the important contribution of literature to the creation of new possibilities and new realities, to the making of new worlds:

I have tried to make the case that the function of literature as art is to open us to dilemmas, to the hypothetical,
to the range of possible worlds that a text can refer to. I
have used the term "to subjunctivize," to render the world
less fixed, less banal, more susceptible to recreation. Literature subjunctivizes, makes strange, renders the obvious
less so, the unknowable less so as well, matters of value
more open to reason and intuition. Literature, in this spirit, is an instrument of freedom, lightness, imagination,
and yes, reason. It is our only hope against the long gray
night. (1986, p. 159)

In a similar vein, we would like to rest our case for a therapy that
incorporates narrative and written means. We have found these
means to be of very great service in the introduction of new perspectives and to a "range of possible worlds," to the privileging of
vital aspects of lived experience in the "recreation" of unfolding
stories, in enlisting persons in the re-authoring of their lives and
relationships.

In this book we have presented but a small sample of narrative
means that have contributed to a therapy that we believe to be an
instrument of liberty, one that has provided a great deal of hope
for persons against what might otherwise be "the long gray night."

References

Anderson, H., & Goolishian, H. A. (1988). Human systems as linguistic systems: Preliminary and evolving ideas about the implications for clinical theory. *Family Process, 27*(4), 371–393.

Barlow, C., Epston, D., Murphy, M., O'Flaherty, L., & Webster, L. (1987). In memory of Hatu (Hayden) Barlow 1973–1985. *Case Studies, 2*(2), 19–37.

Bateson, G. (1972). *Steps to an ecology of mind.* New York: Ballantine Books.

Bateson, G. (1979). *Mind and nature: A necessary unity.* New York: Dutton.

Brooks, P. (1984). *Reading for the plot: Design and intention in narrative.* New York: Random House.

Bruner, E. (1986a). Ethnography as narrative. In V. Turner, & E. Bruner (Eds.), *The anthropology of experience.* Chicago: University of Illinois Press.

Bruner, E. (1986b). Experience and its expressions. In V. Turner, & E. Bruner (Eds.), *The anthropology of experience.* Chicago: University of Illinois Press.

Bruner, J. (1986). *Actual minds, possible worlds.* Cambridge, MA: Harvard University Press.

Bruner, J. (1987). Life as narrative. *Social Research, 54*(1).

Burton, A. (1965). The use of written productions in psychotherapy. In L. Pearson (Ed.), *Written communications in psychotherapy.* Springs, IL: C. C. Thomas.

Cecchin, G. (1987). Hypothesizing, circularity, and neutrality revisited: An invitation to curiosity. *Family Process, 26*(4), 405–413.

Chafe, W. (1985). Linguistic differences produced by differences between speaking and writing. In D. R. Olson, N. Torraru, & A. Hildycrill (Eds.), *Literacy, language and learning.* Cambridge, MA: Cambridge University Press.

Chatwin, B. (1988). *The songlines.* London: Picador.

Durrant, M. (1985). Bowling out fears — Test victory for double description. *Dulwich Centre Review.*

Durrant, M. (1989). Temper taming: An approach to children's temper problems — revisited. *Dulwich Centre Newsletter,* Autumn.

Epston, D. (1983). Cheryl-Anne's new autobiography. *Australian Journal of Family Therapy, 4*(4), 259–261.

Epston, D. (1984a). A story in a story. *Australian Journal of Family Therapy, 5*(2), 146–150.

Epston, D. (1984b). Guest Address, 4th Australian Family Therapy Conference. *Australian Journal of Family Therapy, 5*(1), 11–16.

Epston, D. (1985a). A fair exchange. *Australian & New Zealand Journal of Family Therapy, 6*(2), 114–115.

Epston, D. (1985b). The family with the malediction. *Australian & New Zealand Journal of Family Therapy, 6*(3), 175–176.

Epston, D. (1986a). Writing your biography. *Case Studies, 1*(1), 13–18.

Epston, D. (1986b). Competition or co-operation? *Australian & New Zealand Journal of Family Therapy, 7*(2), 119–120.

Epston, D. (1986c, February). Counter-dreaming. *Dulwich Centre Newsletter.*

Epston, D. (1988). *One good revolution deserves another. Case Studies, 3*(2): 45–60.

Epston, D. (1989). Temper tantrum parties: Saving face, losing face, or going off your face. *Dulwich Centre Newsletter,* Autumn.

Epston, D., & Brock, P. (1984). A strategic approach to an extreme feeding problem. *Australian Journal of Family Therapy, 5*(2), 111–116.

Epston, D., & Whitney, R. (1988). The story of Dory the cat. *Australian & New Zealand Journal of Family Therapy, 9*(3), 172–173.

Foucault, M. (1965). *Madness and civilization: A history of insanity in the age of reason.* New York: Random House.

Foucault, M. (1973). *The birth of the clinic: An archeology of medical perception.* London: Tavistock.

Foucault, M. (1979). *Discipline and punish: The birth of the prison.* Middlesex: Peregrine Books.

Foucault, M. (1980). *Power/knowledge: Selected interviews and other writings.* New York: Pantheon Books.

Foucault, M. (1982). The subject and power. In H. Dreyfus & P. Rabinow, (Eds.), *Michael Foucault: Beyond structuralism and hermeneuties.* Chicago: University of Chicago Press.

Foucault, M. (1984a). *The history of sexuality.* Great Britain: Peregrine Books.

Foucault, M. (1984b). Space, knowledge and power. In P. Rabinow (Ed.), *The Foucault reader.* New York: Pantheon.

Foucault, M. (1984c). Nietzsche, geneology, history. In P. Rabinow (Ed.), *The Foucault reader.* New York: Pantheon.

Garfinkel, H. (1956). Conditions of successful degradation ceremonies. *American Journal of Sociology, 61,* 420–424.

Geertz, C. (1976). From nature's point of view: On the nature of anthropological understanding. In K. Basso & H. Selby (Eds.), *Meaning in anthropology.* Albuquerque, NM: University of New Mexico Press.

Geertz, C. (1983). *Local knowledge: Further essays in interpretive anthropology.* New York: Basic Books.

Geertz, C. (1986). Making experiences, authoring selves. In V. Turner & E. Bruner (Eds.), *The anthropology of experience.* Chicago: University of Illinois Press.

Gergen, M. M., & Gergen, K. J. (1984). The social construction of narrative accounts. In K. J. Gergen & M. M. Gergen (Eds.), *Historical social psychology.* Hillsdale: Lawrence Erlbaum Associates.

Goffman, E. (1961). *Asylums: Essays in the social situation of mental patients and other inmates.* New York: Doubleday.

Goffman, E. (1974). *Frame analysis.* New York: Harper.

Harre, R. (1985). Situational rhetoric and self-presentation. In J. P. Forgen (Ed.), *Language and social situations.* New York: Springer-Verlag.

Irigaray, L. (1974). *Speculum de l'autre femme.* Paris: Minuit.

Iser, W. (1978). *The act of reading.* Baltimore, MD: Johns Hopkins University Press.

Meadows, J. (1985). Video & Audio Review. *Australian & New Zealand Journal of Family Therapy, 6*(2), 117–118.

Menses, G., & Durrant, M. (1986). Contextual residential care: The application of the principles of cybernetic therapy to the residential treatment of irresponsible adolescents and their families. *Dulwich Centre Review.*

Munro, C. (1987). White and the cybernetic therapies: News of differences. *Australian & New Zealand Journal of Family Therapy, 8*(4), 183–192.

Myerhoff, B. (1982). Life history among the elderly: Performance, visibility and remembering. In J. Ruby (Ed.), *A crack in the mirror: Reflexive perspectives in anthropology.* Philadelphia: University of Pennsylvania Press.

Rabinow, P. (1984). *The Foucault reader.* New York: Pantheon.

Ricoeur, P. (1980). Narrativetime. *Critical Inquiry,* Autumn, p. 171.

Spender, D. (1983). *Women of ideas: And what men have done to them.* London: Ark.

Stubbs, M. (1980). *Language and literacy: The socialinguistics of reading and writing.* London: Routledge, Kegan, Paul.

Tomm, K. (1987). Interventive interviewing: Part II, Reflexive questioning as a means to enable self healing. *Family Process, 26,* 167–84.

Tomm, K. (1989). Externalizing problems and internalizing personal agency. *Journal of Strategic and Systemic Therapies.*

Turner, V. (1969). *The ritual process.* New York: Cornell University Press.

Turner, V. (1974). *Drama, fields and meta-phor.* New York: Cornell University Press.

Turner, V. (1986). Dewey, Dilthey, and drama: An essay in the anthropology of experience. In V. Turner & E. Bruner (Eds.), *The anthropology of experience.* Chicago: University of Illinois Press.

Turner, B. S., & Hepworth, M. (1982). *Confessions: Studies in deviance in religion*. London: Routledge, Kegan, Paul.

van Gennep (1960). *The rites of passage*. Chicago: University of Chicago Press.

White, M. (1984). Pseudo-encopresis: From avalanche to victory, from vicious to virtuous cycles. *Family Systems Medicine, 2*(2).

White, M. (1985). Fear busting and monster taming: An approach to the fears of young children. *Dulwich Centre Review*.

White, M. (1986a). Negative explanation, restraint and double description: A template for family therapy. *Family Process, 25*(2).

White, M. (1986b). Anorexia nervosa: A cybernetic perspective. In J. Elka-Harkaway (Ed.), *Eating disorders and family therapy*. New York: Aspen.

White, M. (1986c). Family escape from trouble. *Case Studies, 1*(1).

White, M. (1987, Spring). Family therapy and schizophrenia: Addressing the 'In-the-corner lifestyle.' *Dulwich Centre Newsletter*.

White, M. (1988, Winter). The process of questioning: A therapy of literary merit? *Dulwich Centre Newsletter*.

Index